The Plight of the African-American Male

An Informative Guide to Healing and Restoration

Larry McCullum, MDiv

authorHOUSE®

AuthorHouse™
1663 Liberty Drive
Bloomington, IN 47403
www.authorhouse.com
Phone: 1-800-839-8640

© 2009 Larry McCullum, MDiv. All rights reserved.

No part of this book may be reproduced, stored in a retrieval system, or transmitted by any means without the written permission of the author.

First published by AuthorHouse 8/17/2009

ISBN: 978-1-4490-0655-6 (e)
ISBN: 978-1-4490-0656-3 (sc)
ISBN: 978-1-4490-0657-0 (hc)

Library of Congress Control Number: 2009907600

Printed in the United States of America
Bloomington, Indiana

This book is printed on acid-free paper.

Contents

Acknowledgments vii

Introduction ix

On Minorities and These United States of America 1

The State of African-American Men 7

Identifying the Cause not the Problem 13

Healing not Fixing 23

A Method for Obtaining Wholeness 27

Educate to Integrate not Assimilate 49

Restoration 56

Are today's Mega Churches Effective in Liberating the African-American Male and Restoring Him unto our families and communities? (Case Study) 62

On Racism and Human Sexuality 81

Self-inflicted Wounds (Our attitude towards sexuality and gender identity-based cultures) 86

Epilogue 105

Appendix 1 107

Appendix 2 108

References 112

Additional Works Conferred 115

Acknowledgments

Having lived a life full of challenges, opportunities, and transitions that have served to shape, mold and mature me, I have learned to thank God for the benefits of life and to be most thankful for those He has brought me into relationship with.

In particular, I am blessed and most grateful for the birth of my children, Cymora, Alexis, and Larry, Jr. They are the precious jewels of my life over which God alone has given me stewardship. I love them dearly, for they are the breath within my lungs and the smile upon my countenance. They are the motivation to be all that God has called me to be, for I understand that the blessings of the father will pass along to the children.

I thank God for my soul mate, Chanelle McCullum, who continues to be a refreshing and enduring support. Our love is eternal.

I thank God for the exploratory years of my life as well, for it was through these years that I came to know Him as my shield and my fortress.

I acknowledge foremost, my precious and dearest mother, Louise McCullum, who demonstrated the meaning of a "living epistle". It was through her silent prayers and informing gazes that cause me to continue to press forward through the oppressive forces of rural Mississippi and to ultimately live a life that she and my ancestors deserve.

I acknowledge and bless God always for my biological Father upon this earth, John McCullum, Jr. who, through his resilience and determination to be a provider for his entire family, taught me the importance of being there for my family as well.

I acknowledge and give honor to my spiritual father and pastor; Bishop Donald Hilliard, Jr. who has consistently demonstrated integrity both in and out of the pulpit. You have impacted my life tremendously. May God bless you for your sacrifices, tremendously!

I give honor to the one who thought it not robbery to mentor me in the things of God, while being careful to keep me humble, the honorable Dr. Pastor B. Glover-Williams.

I acknowledge with great gratitude, my brother in Christ for life, Charles Stansbury, who guided me through the process of publishing this manuscript. I owe you one!

Lastly, I thank God for a whole host of friends and acquaintances, who poked, prodded, pressed, and pulled me in every direction; for through it all the contents of this book was made manifest.

> God bless you all mightily

Introduction

The following objectives will serve as a guideline for the reader to navigate through this book. I encourage the reader to approach this book with an open mind, for in doing so, the confines of socio-behavioral construction will be overcome and a space for dialogue and critical engagement will be created.

Although the majority of this book can be easily comprehended and digested by the lay reader, there are sections that contain case studies and terminology that requires critical comprehension on an intellectual level. These sections notwithstanding, it is my hope that the reader will be able to grasp its content and engage it in such a way that will assist him/her in forging new inroads towards understanding the plight of the African American male.

This book will:

- Provide a pathway for understanding the plight of the African American male and his impact on the family and community

- Provide information on the current state of the African American male within borders of these United States

- Provide historical insight into the importance of the African American family and community

- Examine behaviors that are devastating to the African American male, his family and community

- Provide methodology that will assist in bringing about change in healing and restoration

- Underscore the power of education in empowering and restoring the prominence of the African American male, his family and community

- Analyze the effectiveness of today's "mega churches" in bringing wholeness, spiritual maturity and healing to the African American family and community

- Provide studies, methodologies and anecdotes to help the reader clearly and effectively assess issues impacting the African American male, his family and community

- Approach the issues from practical, philosophical, psychological, and theological perspectives

- Provoke the reader to assess his state of being and his role in contributing to rebuild the African American family and community

- Create a space for dialogue regarding the plight of the African American male

On Minorities And These United States of America

"America, the land of the free, home of the brave." "America, the land of opportunity." These and other slogans are the catch phrases that lure so many across the borders of capitalistic United States of America. The United States of America was and is seen as "the way up"; "the promised land"; "the land of opportunity" for not only the poor in third world countries, but for the poor in most European countries as well. America, the land of opportunity, is for many the answer to economic disparity within their homelands, the way to move up the social scale, the way to pull themselves up by their "bootstraps".

In search of a hope for a brighter future, so many, particularly those who lived near the shores of these United States, risk their lives in make-shift boats, attempting to cross dangerous waters in an effort to reach this purported land of opportunity. However, what is the reality for those who reach its borders and seek to integrate into its society? For the majority, the hope of realizing the American dream diminishes, and many are left with nowhere to turn. They are trapped between the land that was and the land promised, for they begin shortly after their arrival to experience the sunken reality of it all. Opportunity exists but at what cost and for what ethnic group?

For those immigrants who have risked much to find new found freedom in this land of opportunity, here are some questions for you: have you forgotten, have you not been taught, or are you unaware of the methods the discoverers' of this new found land used to elevate themselves to economic promise? Are you unaware, that the same country you seek to contribute your talents and service to (in hopes of financial reward) is the same country that has a history of enslaving and oppressing minorities? Are you unaware that the very country in which you seek refuge is the very cause of you having to do so? This country, through its various policies and treaties, works systematically to ensure that underprivileged nations are underdeveloped and the result is you having to leave your homeland in search a better life.

This new found land, America, is a construct arising from a patriarchal, imperialistic culture that has sought to dominate and exert its will on the entire world throughout history. From Alexander the Great to Napoleon, from Columbus to Cortez and from Monroe to Bush, the posture of this nation has been to search out and dominate all in the name of their God, and in search of wealth and riches at any cost. "Take it by force" has been their historical mantra.

The unfortunate truth faced by immigrants to this nation, specifically immigrants of color, is that the land of opportunity and freedom is really a robust system that maintains wealth for a few white men and their families. The unfortunate reality is that the richest twenty percent in America owns over eighty percent of all wealth. This unequal distribution of wealth indicates a major social inequality for eighty percent of U.S. households. It is evident from these statistics that there exists a system within America that promotes the rich and denigrates the poor working class.

For minority Americans born within the borders of the United States, classism, racism, sexism, or any other form of systematic oppression is not a surprise. For so many grueling years, generations of Americans have been subjected to hard labor amidst racist and discriminative laws and post chattel slavery laws that resulted in families etching out a meager living, while the elite wealthy white Americans work within a system that is designed to create and maintain generational wealth. History tells of chattel slavery, transferrable human property, i.e. transferable wealth from generation to generation for white slave owners and it speaks of colonialism and its devastating effects upon the native people of this territory. History also speaks of Jim Crow Laws, Union discrimination and racism systematically designed to oppress the poor while shielding the white dominant class. America, throughout history, has been a purported land of opportunity for all, but at its core dwells a heartless, selfish, insensitive imperialistic system of oppression and greed that has no regard for the common good.

As years passed, new technologies were developed, and new means of ensuring the socio-economic position of the wealthy were sought out. As though the political, legal and corporate disparities in this country alone were not enough, this system of economic disparity seeks to exercise its control on global markets as well. In an article entitled *"The ABCs of The Global Economy"* by The Dollars and Sense Collective, March/April 2000, chapter 3; U.S. corporations are on a corporate offensive. "Corporate America is now going after profits in the international economy. Instead of producing goods in the U.S. to export, they moved more and more toward producing goods overseas..." This strategy not only has a major impact on the U.S. economy, in that the poor struggling underclass of America will struggle even more through loss of job opportunities, but it also impacts the economies of the countries in which these countries seek to operate. More often than not, these corporations seek to protect their interest by compelling governments to "tax, regulate and subsidize foreign businesses exactly as they would their local businesses," for any losses in profit due to changes in public policy. U.S. corporations in international markets controlling international governments resemble colonialism and imperialism, irrespective of the fact that it is being done under the guise of capitalism.

It has been made clear that a highly organized system exists within America, designed to benefit the wealthy, while oppressing the less fortunate. But, how can it be stopped or at the very least circumvented? The upper class in America controls the nation's wealth and, by direct correlation, they control the nation's power. They either hold positions of power or indirectly have influence over positions of power. As long as this unequal distribution of power remains in place, the hopes of creating a fair and equal opportunity system for all American's remain bleak.

I believe the hope of a better future for minorities lie in education. More minorities are graduating from college now than in times past. With increases in minority education, along with a steady rise in the minority population, it is projected that there will be a reversal in the nation's demographics in the near future. It has been projected that by the middle of the twenty-first century, the minorities of today will be the majority of tomorrow. Not only will the shear numbers increase demographically, but also the number of these individuals educated will increase as well, resulting in the influx of much more empowered minority groups into the marketplace. Undoubtedly, these groups will be poised to contribute to the economy and to society. But, will this be enough to shift the existing power structure? It is not income alone that will close socio-economic gaps. Income must be accompanied by the building of wealth. Wealth is transferrable and it will serve to maintain higher social positions for those who inherit it. Therefore, along with the demographic paradigm shift that is to occur during the twenty-first century, a corresponding strategy for increasing wealth must be employed in order for any true gains to be realized.

Additionally, there will be a need for organized groups to lead the transformation that will occur. The groups must be unselfish and have a spirit of sacrifice. They must work for the common and greater good of the people. Historically, within minority communities, the church has assumed this role. But, I'm not so sure that it should be necessarily the role of the church to help correct socio-economic injustices that are prevalent in America or should it be? On the other hand, one could ask, perhaps "Is it solely the role of political groups to advocate change within a socio-political system?" I strongly believe that in order to tackle such a monster, a strategic allegiance between these two groups and other support groups, is required. Relighious groups through education, emancipation, and empowerment measures can assist families in their efforts to raise their identity IQs as well as to exhort an otherwise disparate group to step out and reach for more.

Political groups can continue to fight for laws and social programs that benefit the lower classes within America, as well as providing opportunities for equalized wealth throughout class groups. However, even with a coalition of religious and political organizations, and an impending paradigm shift in the nation's demographics, the task is great. However, to sit by idly and do nothing while the wealthy get wealthier is not an option. The minority groups of tomorrow must continue to prepare themselves academically, as well as to align themselves in a way that is insistent on liberation, economic freedom and equal opportunity for all.

I have taken the time to explain the bright attractions of America to you as well as lay a foundation of the forces at work within America that contradicts those bright attractions. I have not only attempted to shed some light on the crisis that exists within these United States of America for minorities at large, but I have attempted to lay the foundation to explore further the travesty of this crisis for a certain group in particular—the African American male and his community—for to deal with all of the minority groups within America will be a rather robust undertaking.

Please read further as I begin to chip away at the forces that hinder the African American male from truly integrating into American society, as well as explore ways to restore the African male to his prominent place with family, community, and within the nation.

The State of African American Men

Innate to and subconsciously working within every African-American male is the spirit of the African ideals regarding family and community. The tradition of African people is one that embraces close-knit communities where everyone, the African male in particular, is expected to live a life that sacrifices for the greater good of the community. The close, yet expanding family unit is essential, but it exists so that all might contribute to the betterment of the greater community. For the African family, it can be said that the more the merrier.

This African ideal regarding family and community has been transferred to or inherited by their descendants. It is encoded within the DNA, if you will, of the African-American male that forms for him the ideals of family and the importance of community. The African-American male by nature has an attitude of reverence towards family and community. For the African-American male, the family and community are the places where his identity is established and affirmed. It is within the family and community where his net worth is gained and shared. Traditionally, the role of man within the family has placed him as a central figure. Therefore, it is expected and understood that his role within the family and community has to be one in which he actively contributes in a positive way. It should be understood that the male was to live a life of sacrifice for the greater good of the community. For the African American male, there is an innate desire to belong to something greater that has traversed generations and lands. This desire begins with, is supported by, and has been influenced by African tradition, and by the African cultural belief system regarding family.

God almighty has created humankind to exist in relationship. The need to belong to a group or social structure is written upon the hearts of man by the creative finger of God. This notion of existing within community is evidenced throughout biblical passages, and has been studied by many sociologist and psychologists. The mother must bond with her newborn child, or else there exists a chance that the child may be emotionally and/or mentally underdeveloped. (Bowlby 1958) In addition to mother-child bonding, the father plays an active role in the development of the child, which is equally important. The absence of the father within the family structure has been shown to have devastating consequences on the child's development, and may result in destructive behavior during adolescence and/or adulthood. (National Center for Children in Poverty) It is therefore within the human experience, the necessity of existing within family structure, for it lends to emotionally and mentally stable progeny. Ingrained in the male's DNA, particularly the African-American male's DNA, is the need to belong and exist in relationship, which is critical to the emotional, intellectual and psychological health of his offspring, and ultimate the family and community.

The African-American male has both a historical and present need to belong and operate within a tightly knit social system. His very existence within the community was sacrificial, and as such, he needed to contribute to the community and not be overly concerned with individual accomplishments, unless those accomplishments would have a positive impact on the community as a whole. Nancy Body Franklin in her book "Black Families in Therapy—Understanding the African American Experience" (2003), states, regarding the African American male, "to be human was to belong to the whole community". She goes on to say that the African male was largely concerned with doing "not something for the betterment of the individual, but rather something for the community of which the individual was an integral part". It is indeed ingrained in the DNA of African American men not only to exist within community but also to contribute richly to it.

If we were to consider this family belief system from a spiritual perspective, we would perhaps conclude that existence apart from community, or to be excluded from community and not being allowed the opportunity to actively contribute to community, has grave and devastating consequences. If we were to reflect on what I call the *expulsion from the garden principle*, we will begin to uncover spiritually the impact of expulsion and exclusion and how it has contributed to the breakdown of the African-American male's positive role in society.

The African-American male's progenitor, Adam was expelled from the garden (or the family of God) due to disobedience. He and his wife were disobedient to their heavenly father and subsequently had to experience devastating consequences of that disobedience—expulsion from the garden. As a result of the first man and woman's disobedience and subsequent expulsion, the human condition became one of depravity and in need of restoration. Yes, God had a plan to restore them into His family, but the process preceding this restoration was devastating. Can you imagine living in pure, unadulterated relationship with God, free of worries, sickness, and death, then you wake up one day, it's all gone, and you are left to fend for yourself? This had to be devastating to Adam and his descendants. Subsequent to this, the African-American males' more recent ancestor was taken by force out of his family and community, and thrust into slavery and therefore was expelled from his garden; his homeland of Africa. This travesty, the transatlantic slave trade, would set in motion a chain of traumatic events that would have an impact on its progeny. Biblical history records the devastation as this: *"...I the LORD thy God am a jealous God, visiting the iniquity of the fathers upon the children unto the third and fourth generation of them that hate me."* (KJV) Today, because of post modern racism and discrimination, the African American male is still being expelled, and this expulsion from his garden leaves behind a trail of devastation that is evident within the present state of his family and community.

The African American male is being expelled emotionally, mentality and physically from his family and community, and is prohibited from actively participating or contributing to American society as a whole. African American men are disproportionally incarcerated, unemployed and underemployed, and above all, disproportionally compensated for equal services conducted in equal positions as their Caucasian counterparts. They are and have been systematically expelled from the garden in which the American majority so freely participates. This is what I call the *expulsion from the garden principle*, and the African American male has always experienced expulsion throughout the ages. Utilizing this principle of expulsion, one can see the historical cause leading up to the present devastation of the African American family and community. This principle allows one to better understand the cause of the family and community breakdown, and begins to draw strict attention to its originals. Additionally, one can begin to see the importance of family and community and hopefully deduce that if the African American male is not afforded the opportunity to make a positive contribution to his family and community as a means of survival, he will find a way to contribute if not positive then negatively.

This *expulsion from the garden principle* is evidenced by a sense of aggravation; anxiety and anger that often is exhibited by African American men and the impact of these potentially dangerous emotions have wreaked havoc on the African American male and his family and community. It has resulted in an increase in crime, an increase in African American suicides and a fundamental breakdown in the belief system that is ingrained within him. Thus the biblical proverb: *"The fathers eat sour grapes, and the children's teeth are set on edge"* (KJV) is likely to have become flesh once again in the lives of God's people.

According to the U.S. Census Bureau, National Center for Health Statistics, Americans for Divorce Reform (www.divorcemag.com/statistics/statsUS.html), fatherless homes account for 63% of youth suicides, 90% of homeless/runaway children, 85% of children with behavior problems, 71% of high school dropouts, 85% of youths in prison, well over 50% of teen mothers. Additionally, 24% of the American population has never been married, indicating a major shift in the nation's attitude toward marriage and family.

In addition, there are startling statistics that point to African Americans. African Americans (28.5%) are about six times more likely than their Caucasian counterparts (4.4%) to be admitted to prison during their lifetime (U.S. Department of Justice). Based on current rates of incarceration, an estimated 7.9% of African American males compared to 0.7% of Caucasian males, will enter State or Federal prison by the time they are age 20, and 21.4% of African American males versus 1.4% of Caucasian males, will be incarcerated by age 30 (U.S. Department of Justice). The National Institute of Drug Abuse estimated that while 12 percent of drug users are African Americans, they make up nearly 50 percent of all drug possession arrests in the U.S. This is the state of African American men, and we must work through the power of Christ that worketh in us, to take direct action and restore the African American man to his place of prominence, promise and prosperity.

Identifying the cause not the problem

Too often, we see an individual demonstrating destructive behavior either towards themselves or towards someone else. Traditional thought and response to such behavior would result in attributing blame to the individual observed demonstrating the behavior. The natural verbal response or conscious thought elicited would probably be something like, *"what's his problem?"* Due to social construction, we often take a *"point the finger"* or *"place the blame"* approach to every situation that does not fit neatly into what we feel is normal or acceptable in our world. Rarely, do we stop to think beyond what he/she has observed. We, for whatever reason, choose not to consider the action any further, and in so doing, we label the person observed solely as the victimizer when quite possibly they might be both the *victimizer and victimized*.

I'd like to share a childhood story with you, if I may. Growing up in the rural South, engulfed in oppressive systemic racial discrimination, I have experienced many hardships. I have experienced personally the right hook of a segregated South that strikes with evil intent those not a part of the socio-economic majority. I have watched with my very eyes, the arm of injustice reach out with crippling fervor to pull the legs out from under those who, with their very arms, once held them as though a mother weaning her newborn child. I have watched with perplexity, the feet of southern power structure stomp the face and body of those who looked kindly on them, the ones who used their God-given bodies to farm land that was once theirs, but now taken away from them. These are the emotional scars of an oppressive South within whose borders I grew up, the memories of which I would like to share briefly with you.

I recall first hand, in the early seventies, being bused from an all black (pardon me, the nomenclature of the time branded us colored), all colored school twenty-five miles in the opposite direction of the colored school, in which I had attended from my home. This was done all in the name of integration, and was the result of the Civil Rights Movement that was designed to make the world a better place.

These times were hard! I remember the first day at this all white school. My brother, one of my sisters and I, got off the now integrated bus, having withstood the stares and grimaces of those that resisted change. I was seven at the time, my brother was nine, and my sister was eight. We stepped off the bus and made our way to our respective classes. The day went relatively smoothe, but it was the ride home that was to mark this day, a day that would be etched in my mind and the minds of my siblings forever.

On the way home, my brother and sister did not expect the ride home to be any different than the ride to school that morning. However, little did we know that while we were riding, one of the older white boys on the bus began calling us names and shouting expletives. The atmosphere on the bus had changed from the stares and grimaces we faced on the ride to school, to one of hostility. One of the older white boys decided to take aggressive action against my slightly older brother. The

The Plight of the African-American Male

white boy was about sixteen or so and my brother was only nine. The white boy attacked my brother, as my sister and I watched, unable to do or say anything for we were paralyzed by shock. Undoubtedly fueled by socially constructed uncontrolled racial hatred towards blacks and the fear of social change, the white boy stomped my brother's face with combat boots, and continued to stomp him. Blood was everywhere! The bus driver, a white person, didn't react to the beating at all. He/she (as I can't remember the gender of the driver) just kept driving as though nothing was happening. I couldn't continue to look. I was helpless, scared, and traumatized. I turned my face to the back of the bus until the attack was over. The attack didn't cease until the driver came to the house of the older white boy that was doing the beating. I caught another glimpse of the attacker after hearing the driver wish him a good afternoon, and seeing him through the bus' rear window as we drove off. My brother lifted himself off of the bus floor in silence and just sat there until we arrived home.

As we arrived home, my mother and father were astonished. They didn't know what to do! That night, I heard my older sisters and brothers planning to resolve the situation on the next morning. I had twelve brothers and sisters enrolled in school at that time, and they were very protective of their younger siblings. They had planned to resolve the situation with violence. I listened intently, taking it all in and meditating on it throughout the night. Little did I know, my soul was being imprinted, my emotional well being was being scarred, and my life was entering a stage of fragmentation, due to the painful events that had transpired and that had set off a dangerously vicious pattern of violence that a young seven year old, or any adolescent for that matter, would have difficulty rebounding from. We were products of the time; victims of a cruel society that was bent on resisting change, and unless emotional help lie somewhere in the future, life was to be filled with internal struggles that would not complicate our lives, but those of our not-to-distant families.

The next morning all of my brothers and sisters boarded the bus. Everyone was waiting for the older white boy, who attacked my brother, to board but he never did. His father had taken him to school that day in fear of retaliation. His father was trying to protect him. Well, that didn't stop my brothers and sisters. When the bus arrived at the now integrated school, one of my siblings recognized the boy from a distance and all of my siblings ran after him. The boy ran into the principal's office hoping to find protection, but that didn't help. That day, the boy and the principal all suffered at the hands of my siblings. The method of corporate nonviolent social change had developed within it a Malcolm Xism. The nonviolent social change movement of the time had resulted in integration of the schools, but a "by any means necessary" method had resolved an attack of violence perpetrated against a helpless colored child, by a white adolescent socially conditioned for racial hatred.

Because of this incident, the family—my brother in particular—were never the same. We all remember it like it was yesterday. My brother, the victim of the violence is now emotionally scared. He is outraged when anyone, white, black, brown, or yellow, according to his perception, tries to undermine or invade his personal space. He has spent a lifetime trying to adjust to those who run big business. He has spent a lifetime trying to establish himself as a positive contributor to society, and now being a father, he has tried hard to raise his children in a way that moves them towards emotional wholeness, all the while, holding in memory the painful past of his childhood. He never received counseling.

He never received any psychotherapy. He simply repressed the pain, as did I. We simply locked the incident away in the deep, dark crevices of our mind, only to visit them occasionally, but to have them played out continually within our personal lives. We were victimized that day, and because of that victimization, we became victimizers. I am not condoning our behavior, but what I am saying is that sometimes you can't know the reason for destructive behavior just by observing it. You must know the history of the person exhibiting that behavior, and if you care enough seek to get an understanding, for you never know God might want to use you to bring about healing in their lives. Let's not *point the finger* or merely *assign blame*! Let's seek to understand!

This *"point the finger"* or *"place the blame"* does not open pathways for understanding behavior, it merely assigns blame, all the while leaving the person demonstrating the negative behavior, to continue that behavior uncorrected. The approach of assigning blame merely seeks to categorize behavior. After all, we exist in a world that cannot function unless it assigns labels.

Diverse groups of people cannot exist solely as diverse members of the human race because society must place a label on their diversity. Blacks must be labeled as one thing, whites must be labeled as another thing and so forth. Our preoccupation with labels obstructs our ability to comprehend the larger problem. It stops progress before it ever begins; never giving the *victimizer/victimized* an opportunity to be understood. In the end we write the individual off, and they eventually end up trapped in our criminal justice system, rarely finding their way back into mainstream society. As we all should know, our criminal justice system is not a fix. It is merely a holding cell system where the unwanted, disenfranchised, misunderstood and disavowed are kept, so that mainstream America may live in a false sense of security. We are all called to do something greater for all humankind! We are to not simply cast blame, but work together to help our fellow brethren, and to heal the wounds of the *victimizer/victimized* that he might be re-acclimated into the community.

I am not suggesting that one should try to understand and subsequently attempt to fix every problem or every negative behavior. But what I am suggesting is that we not be so quick to pass judgment, without first really finding the underlying cause of the behavior, for understanding opens the pathways towards healing.

Renown psychiatrist Murray Bowen presents an interesting methodology for assessing family dynamics, and the stresses present in them. Bowen suggests in his family systems theory that individuals cannot be understood in isolation from one another, but rather as a part of their family, as the family is an emotional unit (Kerr and Bowen 1988). Can you imagine the implications this theory has when placed upon the African American male?

As was stated earlier, the African American males' belief system is one that is rooted within the functional family. Family, to the descendants of African slaves, is more than just the immediate family; it is the community. Therefore, if we apply Bowen's family systems theory to the dysfunctional behavior that presently exists within the African American family, we have a means for examining and understanding their behavior. In doing so, we will be able to develop solutions to the problems affecting them rather than merely assigning blame.

Using the family systems theory to understand the dynamics of African American men provides us with a measure of the devastating impact that slavery, institutionalization, disenfranchisement as well as racial discrimination has had on them. Using this theory, one can begin to understand that what may be driving the imbalance in incarceration rates, test scores, graduation rate, etc., is not the ineptness of the individual in most cases but the social pressures and unfairness that has been pressing in on them since childhood. Racial discrimination, slavery, disenfranchisement, and all of the unfairness imposed upon the African American male, may just well be the root cause of destructive behavior, low self esteem and family dysfunctionality demonstrated within the African American family. The negative images of African Americans is merely the signal that something is wrong within the family structure, and his acting out is a cry for help!

If we were to change this political/social view to a religious/spiritual view, this notion of identifying the cause not the problem can be better understood if we explicate the passage of scripture found in the gospel of Mark chapter 5 that deals with the demon-possessed man.

Mark 5:1-15;18-20 (King James Version)

1 They went across the lake to the region of the Gerasenes. 2 When Jesus got out of the boat, a man with an evil spirit came from the tombs to meet him. 3 This man lived in the tombs, and no one could bind him any more, not even with a chain. 4 For he had often been chained hand and foot, but he tore the chains apart and broke the irons on his feet. No one was strong enough to subdue him. 5 Night and day among the tombs and in the hills he would cry out and cut himself with stones.

6 When he saw Jesus from a distance, he ran and fell on his knees in front of him. 7 He shouted at the top of his voice, "What do you want with me, Jesus, Son of the Most High God? Swear to God that you won't torture

me!" 8 For Jesus had said to him, "Come out of this man, you evil spirit!"

9 Then Jesus asked him, "What is your name?"

"My name is Legion," he replied, "for we are many." 10 And he begged Jesus again and again not to send them out of the area.

11 A large herd of pigs was feeding on the nearby hillside. 12 The demons begged Jesus, "Send us among the pigs; allow us to go into them." 13 He gave them permission, and the evil spirits came out and went into the pigs. The herd, about two thousand in number, rushed down the steep bank into the lake and were drowned.

14 Those tending the pigs ran off and reported this in the town and countryside, and the people went out to see what had happened. 15 When they came to Jesus, they saw the man who had been possessed by the legion of demons, sitting there, dressed and in his right mind; and they were afraid. 18 As Jesus was getting into the boat, the man who had been demon-possessed begged to go with him. 19 Jesus did not let him, but said, "Go home to your family and tell them how much the Lord has done for you, and how he has had mercy on you." 20 So the man went away and began to tell in the Decapolis how much Jesus had done for him. And all the people were amazed.

In this text, we have a man who has been disenfranchised by his community and is now confined to live outside of it in the tombs. The man was viewed by others as a menace. He was thought of as being a problem, and no one took his cries or his fighting as attempts to overcome that which had removed him from society. They only took him to be a menace!

It is not until the end of the passage that we come to realize that this man had a family and he had friends. Nevertheless, no one stopped to understand what was the reason why he was separated from his friends, family, and community. They only tucked him neatly away from society, incarcerated without any immediate remedy for that which ailed him, that is until Jesus came on the scene. The man recognized the solution to the thing(s) that vexed him and took it into his own hands to receive his healing. He broke from the chains that bound him and fell at the feet of salvation—Jesus! Jesus rebuked that which vexed the man and restored him to his friends, family and community!

We see from this text that Jesus was fully aware of the family systems theory, long before Bowen articulated it. He recognized that the destructive behavior that the man was eliciting was not the cause of his condition, but merely the signal that something greater was wrong. Jesus addressed the cause, and in so doing, healed the man so that he might rejoin, contribute and become an integral part of his community.

The African American men of today are in a similar state of depravity! They have been so hardened by societal woes that they are detached and disconnected. They have very little feeling towards humankind and are in a state of survival, which drives them to do any and everything to maintain life. Their hearts have been so hardened by the system of institutionalization, that they are now detached from social norms and moral decency. They have been wronged, abandoned, and raped of hope, that they are walking down a road which to them is devoid of hope. They heap up for themselves treasures that are temporary and unfulfilling. Society continues with its daily business relinquishing these individuals to the judicial system, and isolating itself from the reality that we are all created to function in relationship to each another.

I believe, just like Jesus restored the demoniac to his family and community, the African American man can be restored as well. I know, internally there is a voice that is begging for help. They've heard of Jesus, his history, his word of healing and restoration, but they are now waiting for the word to become flesh in their lives. They are not the problem! They are both the *victimizer/victimized*! Trying to understand the cause of their human condition is a better way to address the state of which they are in, and the family system theory relegates dysfunctional behavior not just to the one who is behaving dysfunctionally. It seeks to understand that the one who is acting out is merely the signal that points to a greater problem.

Healing not Fixing

As we have learned thus far, the African American male, as a result of family and community dysfunctionality and systematic exclusion, has deteriorated to a point where the values, ethics, beliefs and high esteem that were evident within his past legacy are no longer evident. He is yet a fraction of what his ancestors were, and what God has created him to be.

Due to dysfunctionality of the African American family and their communities, the African African males' identity has been lost and his net worth lessened. Yet, if we were to poll the racial majority group within this country, they would say that "everything is find just the way they are". They would say that the progress that was made during the civil rights error was sufficient to allow minorities to function at an acceptable level within society. Jawanza Kunjufu in his book entitled *Black Economics, Solutions for Economic and Community Empowerment* (African American Images, 1991) states: "The issue of civil rights had been a major public concern in the mid 1960s, but it has been declining in popularity for the past 25 years. Surveys show that Whites believe that the problems have been solved..."

In the eyes of the majority some gains without equal status within society is enough for the minority group. Small gains are enough to satisfy the conscience of the descendants of slave owners, and not convict them of the travesty of their past. But for the victimized, it is only an offer of a greater hope that seems to escape them. This offering of little hope frustrates the victimized because it reaggravates wounds that have been slightly healed. It can be compared to putting a band aide over a deep gash in ones heart.

The psyche, soul and heart of the African American male need healing. Every measure to date has been an attempt to fix the social problems working in today's society. The Civil Rights Movement's focus was equal rights! The Back to Africa Movement belief was that the cultures of the majority and minority couldn't coexist. Affirmative Action, although necessary, was an attempt to fix the problem of discrimination. If we are to exist as one nation working together to achieve and promote the American ideals of liberty and justice for all, then we must do more than attempt to fix the problems that afflict its people. We must develop measures, programs and methods that seek to heal the wounds of our past, not simply fix them.

The approach must be therapeutic and not punitive. It must not create emotional unhealthiness in one group, while creating health for the other. The approach cannot offer opportunity for one, while disenfranchising the other. The approach has to be one that works towards the universal good, one that celebrates the unique yet diverse gifts and talents of all that live within its borders.

I believe the measures that we take as a group and as a nation must begin at the simplest level, which is the family. We must work to heal the family and the community. In order to do so, we must understand the dynamics of each individual ethnic group's family. Once we understand, that the African American male's very identity is tied to his family and community, we then can create measures that uniquely address the ills of the African

American family. If this approach is applied to every ethnic group, the result will be the saving of our communities and our nation. We will achieve moral victory, which is a victory that is more everlasting than any judicial or legislative system could ever hope to achieve.

In the biblical book of Malachi 4:6, the Lord makes aware the condition of the family during the prophet's time. There was a breakdown in the family, and it was having a devastating impact on the Israelite community. In this passage, the Lord provides the solution to the problem at hand. He simply declares that before the world comes to an end, I will turn the hearts of the fathers to the children, and the hearts of the children to their fathers, and if I don't the devastation will get worse.

Malachi 4:6 (KJV)

"Behold, I will send you Elijah the prophet before the coming of the great and dreadful day of the Lord. And he will turn the hearts of the fathers to the children, and the hearts of the children to their fathers, lest I come and strike the earth with a curse."

As we can see from the text, God delineates the importance of family and its contribution to a positive community. In my mind and in my heart, there is nothing greater than what God says about a matter. Therefore, the solution to the ills affecting the African American male and his family and community, is to provide healing to the hearts of the fathers and children, i.e. the family. Once we achieve this, the healing will begin to take place! Once we develop and implement measures that integrate and restore the African American male to his rightful place within his family and community, then it will have an effect that will be transforming to not only his community, but to the nation.

Bishop Donald Hilliard, Jr in his book "Somebody Say Yes", makes the following statement: "We are called by God to heal the fever that's rampant in our family and in families across the land. He wants us to use our talents, our time, and our treasure to make a difference in this world!" As one can see, Bishop sees the role of every Christian as one that works to restore the family.

My father in the gospel and mentor in this power book lends credence to, and an inept spiritual understanding of, the cause of the breakdown within the family. He writes, "Many of our precious children are perishing because they are starved for what their fathers should be providing them at home. They are hungry for a daddy's love—his attention, his protection, and his training. In today's society, the absence of a father is one of the most common hindrances to experiencing the abundant life." Bishop Hilliard recognizes that the absence of the father from the family has had devastating affects, which in turn, have generational consequences. The solution for a better society and a better way is to ensure that we promote healing within those who have been disenfranchised, discriminated against, expelled, excluded, and raped of their net worth. We must promote healing and not fixing, if we are to save our families and communities. We are in need of real change, and that change can only come through healing of wounds that drive us towards being a better group of people.

A Method for Obtaining Wholeness

Many people question whether an individual can change his or her behavior. They wonder whether an individual's character traits can really change. These individuals, for whatever reason or another, believe that once a person's personality is constructed at a young age, then it is set for life. This belief that personalities are human constructs is widespread; in fact, many that are highly regarded in the field of academia and research on human behavior support this belief. They underscore this belief when they suggest that by the age of five, a person's personality is constructed. According to Sigmund Freud (a renown psychiatrist and psychoanalyst), we all journey through three stages of personality development, which shapes us for the remainder of our lives. The first stage is the Id (that part of us that allows us to get our needs met). The second stage is the Ego (that part of us that interprets and transfers the reality of every situation and thus keeps in check the Id). The last stage is the Superego (the moral beliefs and ideals that we learn from our parents or caregivers by the age of five). This hypothesis still provides the foundation for how we view human development. Therefore, it is contended that what a person is, and what he or she is predisposed to by age five, shapes his or her personality for the remainder of his life.

We even have certain colloquialisms such as "he's set in his ways", or "you can take the boy out of the country but you can't take the country out of the boy", that serve as verbal attestations to cultural beliefs, which underscore that change in individual personality is highly unlikely and culturally disregarded. These colloquialisms give indication as to how deep the notion of resistance to change is woven into the fabric of American society.

This notion of resistance to behavioral modification that exists among American society, gives rise to many societal complexities that impact a variety of social groups. The belief becomes that all blacks are the same and cannot change; all whites are the same and cannot change, etc. In essence, it gives voice to a nation and culture that is steeped in tradition, making it difficult to move to a society that will equality embrace others.

On the surface, our society professes that change can occur. However, upon close examination, we will find that this profession is only smoke and mirrors. Consider our prison system—termed "correctional facilities". The nomenclature suggests that change of human behavior is plausible. It suggests that our prison system works to correct or change the behavior of those who have demonstrated behavior contrary to the laws of the land. If the incarcerated individual puts his/her time in and follows the rules, then change will occur.

We put millions of dollars into these systems yearly, further lending support that change is possible. While we put millions in support of the system that declares that it can correct behavior, we see no real change in the crime rate (see statistics cited earlier in this work) and an increase in the number of repeat offenders. Correctional facilities—the prison system—are only a façade. Correctional facilities are not a place for positive change. They are merely holding cells, formed to rid society of what they have labeled dysfunctional deviants. The correctional system at work in America is merely a system that underscores our society's resistance to change.

I must say that if we accept the way society has demonstrated its attitude concerning behavior modification, there is not much hope for individuals trapped on the negative end of this social behavior continuum. Individuals who are born in or exposed to particularly non-affirming or negative environments, are, as a consequence, labeled as social misfits with no hopes of changing or ever contributing positively to their families and communities, or to the betterment of themselves. According to society, they are doomed to repeat the same experiences that they have learned from the days of their youth. They are trapped with no choice and with no hope of ever breaking from the chains of their past. They are trapped in a generational cycle of negative behavior.

In fact, our outlook does not provide much hope for anyone seeking to better himself or herself, whether or not they were born into negative environments. Nevertheless, there are individuals out there that embrace diversity—they embrace change—whether its diversity from their family members or friends, diversity from the members of their communities or diversity for the betterment of themselves throughout life. They feel change is inevitable. They feel change is needed. For them, to change is to grow, and growth must occur in order to advance society, in order to better ourselves. Growth must occur or, else, life would cease.

If we ever want our children to achieve greater success than we do, change must be a part of the process. Spiritually speaking, the LORD demonstrated change in the process of human development. The LORD, on one occasion, divested

Himself of all of His glory, became as a little babe, born in a manger, and grew in all wisdom and knowledge. He changed before his family's very eyes to become what God preordained him to be, even before the beginning of time. He grew both in wisdom and in knowledge. His personality exhibited as a young child before the age of twelve, was quite different than what the people of his family and community witnessed once he reached twelve. The passage, "Is this not the carpenters' son?" (Matthew 13:55, KJV) provides credence to this change in personality. Therefore, if God exhibited change through the Son, we as His creation should have a similar desire and an attitude of acceptance towards change for we were created in HIS image.

Now that we have established that there exists within society an attitude of resistance to behavioral modification, how does one who chooses to embrace change succeed in doing so? For the most part, history has shown that individuals that embrace change and have a desire to implement it, believes that sheer will power will do it. We see demonstrations of this belief model year after with the passage of time. Individuals within this belief system make New Year resolutions to change a certain behavior, or resolute to lose weight, or be a nicer person. They work within themselves to achieve the goal of which they have set. Many, if not all of them, will fail at achieving their goal and, as a result, will make the same resolution again before the strike of twelve next New Years Eve, or they will achieve their goal only to relapse into the same behavior or state they were in. Many will become frustrated and will resolve themselves to believe the notion of resistance to change that makes up the fabric of traditional society. Many will give up, never giving effort to positive change again because they failed at their first attempt. The failure for them becomes a once small hurdle that has become an impossible feat, as one attempting mountain climbing for the first time, and choosing a mountain as tall as Mount Everest as his first endeavor. Obviously, this person is doomed for failure, and unless a plausible intervention occurs, disaster might strike and forever change his/her outlook towards attempting anything great again.

Contrary to popular belief, there is a way to achieve change. There is a way to accomplish whatever change you desire in life. There is a way to become a better father, a better person, a better neighbor, a better husband, a better employee or employer. There is a way to lose weight and keep it off. There is a way to control your emotions. There is a way to overcome addictive behavior! There is a way to becoming whatever you choose to embrace or change within your life.

I'd like to share with you three methods that can be used for embracing change in your life. Three practical principles that, if followed, will help to break the cycle of fallacy that asserts that change is not possible; help you overcome the fear of failing, and move you to becoming a successful, transformed, happier, and positive person. It will provide you with indicators on how to recognize the appropriate environment for change, and how to successfully navigate change within your life. If these principles are embraced with a sense of commitment, if you consistently covenant to continue within these precepts for as long as it takes and then some, you will be able to tackle and change anything within your life. You will be able to take the necessary steps that will carry you to your next horizon in life. You will benefit, your family will benefit, and the world at large will benefit, because you have identified the element that you would like to see happen, by way of tackling it and coming out victorious. Your life will have additional meaning and the cycle of repeating the same old ills of old will have been broken. Together, let's take a walk towards embracing the new you.

Remembering

For many of us, life has not been easy. We go through a life that is profuse with negative elements that chip away at our sanity; chip away at our emotion stability; and carving elements of pain and resentment into our soul. In order to handle the many traumatic events that we face, we have developed coping mechanisms. Mechanisms like "what doesn't kill you makes you strong;" "boys don't cry;" and even at the child stage of development, we've concocted statements such as "sticks and stones might break my bones but words will never hurt me".

We have developed these proverbial statements, not so much as a declaration of our toughness to society, but as a coping mechanism that help us navigate through the pain that society has caused us. In fact, we use these proverbial statements as a barrier, a wall to keep us insulated from the pain. We merely hide whatever pain there is behind this area of defense, occasionally giving it a glimpse but never outwardly validating it as a source to be reckoned with. As a result, we live our lives fragmented. We go throughout life as a windowpane, containing many cracks but still holding together. We think that no one can see the cracks, but we are a windowpane made of glass and people see right through. At any moment, with just one more devastating blow to the emotional fabric that is struggling to hold us together, we are poised to crack into many tiny pieces, but our resilience holds us together. We are held together by the hope of a better tomorrow.

This discourse paints the picture of the frailty of humankind. It depicts the emotional needs of practically every individual trying to live life. There is a struggle to maintain, and to make safe navigation through the torrential storms of life. Humankind are survivors, and as such, there is an innate ability to ensure self-preservation. We see elements of this throughout our lives. We morph on the surface, taking on chameleon-like attributes in order to continue on the grand scheme of life.

From a psychological perspective, this discourse depicts the need for a deeper change within individuals. It asserts that life inherently will inflict us all with pain, deep emotional stress that play out violent symphonies within the chorus of our emotional being. This discourse underscores as well the human mechanisms inherent to survival.

Humans will create some level of protection, even one that is merely a façade, in order to continue to survive in the game of life, and while this quest for survival is occurring, deep repression of pain and conflict that could very well lead to emotional and physical infirmity is running its course. If there is hope at all, that is hope for wholeness and healing, we must begin to acknowledge our authentic self. We must recognize and call to memory the ills that lie active but conceal within us. Recall is necessary! Recall is a necessary principle that begins the road towards wholeness and emotional, psychological and physical well-being. We must not repress the pain, but embrace it if we are to be the fearfully and wonderfully made creation that God has intended us to be. Recall must be embraced, for it is therapeutic! There is power in remembering. There is a kinetic energy that is released when I outwardly recall the pain of my past, and it is this kinetic energy that acts as the catalyst toward bringing about a change in my physical, emotional, and psychological world. It is like exhaling after holding your breath for decades (if possible).

I exhort you to take a moment of your time to exercise this principle. Try putting this principle into practice. Do it now.

Think hard. Pull out those repressed events of your childhood, your adolescent years, or even your adulthood. Don't give up, keep trying. As you focus harder and harder and you begin to remember, you will notice that you might become a little uncomfortable, perhaps even aggravated as you recall the painful events of your past. You have begun to uncover the thing that has been lying concealed within. By doing this exercise, you have begun to identify a source of pain and discomfort.

You'll find that you will attempt to rationalize the events of your past or perhaps even question why it had to happen. You'll say to yourself, "why does life or the world at large have to be so tough?" Perhaps you will even try to justify the painful events of your past. Please note that these grappling is merely the initial stages of healing—the initial stages that must be undertaken if you are to bring about change in your life. Be sure not to give up; this process could take days or even months, but what is important is that you begin to recall the repressed events of your past. Try writing them all down so as to not forget any of them, for they all must be dealt with if you are to achieve the wholeness and emotional wealth that you are predestined to walk in. In addition, be sure to write down your feelings about each of the events that you recall, it will help you to identify things that trigger negative emotions or negative behaviors that attempt to resurface. Remembering and writing things down will help ensure that a definite plan for progress is in place. You will be able to look back at the things that you considered giants in your life, and realize that they were merely small stones that you could have tossed away long ago, by addressing them early and never letting them grow into an illusionary giant that was bent on bullying you and destroying your emotional, psychological and physical health.

Reconciliation (to accept something unpleasant or to restore to friendship)

In order to bring about change in your life, the principle of reconciliation or coming to terms with your past must be embraced. One must endeavor to bring disturbing events of their past that have been repressed, as a means of protection, to the forefront. It is critical to face the demons of your past, for only in confronting them will you begin to destroy them. You cannot defeat what you are unwilling to confront.

After recalling the repressed feelings and emotions of your past, it is important that you begin to do the opposite of what you've done over the years. Instead of rejecting those feelings and repressing the painful events, it is now time to embrace them. You must now accept them as a part of your life. It must be understood that those experiences, no matter how negative, have served to shape you and make you what you are today. I know they hurt you and I know that it is most difficult to remember them, but ignoring them does not rid you of them. In fact, by ignoring them you are giving them more power over you than they should have. You must bring them forward and begin to make amends with them, for in so doing, they will become less of a hindrance to your progress.

This is a critical step in order to move forward. It can be equated to overcoming the bully that threatened to take your lunch money during your primary school days. What gave power to the bully, his/her robust stature notwithstanding, was their ability to instill fear within their subjects. Think about it! It is the fear that causes a person to behave contrary to the manner that they may want to exhibit. The bully counts on the ones he/she chooses to intimidate to be afraid of them. Once the fear factor is removed, the bully is neutralized. So, it is with the pains of your past. If they remain repressed, they are placed in the position of the bully, unconfronted, they tug, nag, and poke at your peace and freedom. The bully must be dealt with if you are to go on freely with your life. If not, the bully will continue to feed its own ego by the fear that you are demonstrating, and will keep you trapped, unable to fulfill your full potential in life.

When exposed to the threats of a bully or any other negative stimulus, your body's first reaction is one of preparation—preparation to deal with the situation or run from it. In the scientific world, this phenomenon is commonly known as a flight or fight response. When an animal is confronted with a potentially dangerous situation, a series of biological events are initiated. At the point of confrontation, the animal's biological system readies either him/her to confront the source of threat apparent before he/she fights, or having assessed the situation and realizing (remembering) that perhaps he/she is not equipped to deal with the confrontation at the moment, decides to run (flight). The catalyst for behavior in this response system is the biochemical reactions occurring within the animal. These catalysts will elicit a fight response or a flight response. The system will work to eliminate the immediate danger that the animal is confronted with, as a means of protection and survival. However, the fight or flight response was not designed to be a continuous prolonged event. It was designed to be temporary, merely active longer enough to remove the immediate danger or else it will pose a danger to the very thing it was designed to protect.

As is the case of people who have been traumatized, their response to the trauma is dependent upon this same phenomenon. However, in most cases the flight response has been invoked. Most have repressed the event deeply within their subconscious and they refuse to deal with it. For many, the damage inflicted by the trauma has been allowed to linger for years. The traumatic event happened at an age where they simply were not strong enough or mature enough to handle it. Therefore, the only response that they elicited was the flight phenomenon. The flight response that was elicited at such an early age presented itself as a refusal to recall or remember the event, thereby repressing it as a means of protection from the pain. Unfortunately, this repression of the event may have been a necessary response at the time, but the response was not intended to last forever.

The fight or flight response was devised by God to protect us from harm, temporarily. It was not meant to work continuously, uninterrupted throughout our lives. Our systems simply were not designed for it. It you continue to place unwanted and unwarranted stress on a system, ultimately it will break down. Moreover, break down within the human biological system manifests itself largely as cardiovascular disturbances, e.g. high blood pressure, heart disease, diabetes, etc. It may even manifest itself as psychological imbalances, e.g. depression, loner behavior, bipolarism, etc. all of which pose long-term danger to the one experiencing them.

As in the example of confronting the bully, as well as the natural design of the human system to deal with stress, the painful events of our past exhibited control over us through fear, and the delicateness of our younger years prevented a fight response. Therefore, we succumb to the fear, and our systems chose flight (repression) instead.

Now that we have provided some understanding of why we responded the way we did, we should now understand that it wasn't our fault. We are not responsible for the harm done to us! We didn't do anything wrong! We were not equipped to deal with such traumatic events at such a young age! It's not our fault! Our parents, if present while the event occurred, perhaps would have helped us! After all, it is the responsibility of the parents to provide love and protection to their kids, until which time they are able to handle these events on their own. But something went wrong, and now not only are we impacted, but our parents are, as well as the perpetrators of the injustice. We now are all in need of healing, and part of the solution is to be reconciled to the pain of our past.

In order to be reconciled to our past, we must realize that we are a product of our past. We are, in essence, the sum total of our life experiences. Our past, no matter how painful it may be, has served to shape who we are. Those experiences have either made us stronger or weaker, better or worse, stable or unstable. We are a living past, stamping out and moving towards our future. To deny your past would be to deny a part of you. That event, which we hate to remember, is as much a part of you as the most happy time that you can bring to remembrance! Let's travel back in time to one of my past experiences.

I grew up in a typical large southern family. There were fifteen of which six were boys and nine were girls. We were all close in age, in most cases separated by a little more than a gestation period. My father and mother were together, though my mother had two children from a previous marriage and my father had children from many relationships, at the time unbeknownst to us. My father was a good provider. He worked diligently to ensure that we had food to eat and clothes to wear. My mother was a good nurturer and housewife, who, on occasion, worked for many white families as a housekeeper. Because of their efforts, I grew up unaware that we were poor and barely making, as they say in the South, "ends meet". On the surface, we were the typical African-American family trying to forge a living in a newly political-initiated, but cultural unaccepted integrated South. My father experienced much hardship trying to provide for his functional family, and incurred even much more stress because of the social pressures of the time. I found that he would drink and womanize as a means of coping and dealing with the pressures of his time. He spent very little time at home. He rarely interacted with my mother. She loved him; I could see it in her eyes. I believe, in some twisted and unhealthy way, he loved her as well. However, the way he expressed his love was unhealthy. My father would scream and become angry with my mother and with us for no apparent reason. He would throw things, hurl expletives, and withdraw from my mother. The emotional toil on her must have been unbearable. However, she always kept her silence.

As kids, we couldn't do much. We heard the arguments, saw the callousness my father showed towards our mother, but because of our age, we remained silent. We grew up watching these feats of anger and lack of demonstration of love towards the family. The only time we would see our family demonstrate love is with the aide of alcohol. He would drink and then tell us he loved us! In some strange way, we were glad to hear it for deep down in our souls we also wanted to feel it from him. We received it, but his drinking tarnished it. My mother received the same message, but she would push him away and tell him that she was aware of the outside secretive life that he was living. Nevertheless, she stayed with him. After all, where would an African-American woman with a six-grade education and fifteen kids go! Therefore, the family stayed intact, but we were subjected to the pain of a dysfunctional family. Our souls were scarred! We looked, listened, learned and we kept it all in. With the concealment came resentment, dissociative behavior, and a catalyst towards repeating behavior that would continue to hurt those we professed to love.

I grew up and pushed with extraordinary determination to achieve what the circumstances of my parent's time prohibited them from achieving—a high school diploma. My mother, unfortunately, only had a sixth grade education, and my father a ninth grade education. They were exceptionally smart individuals, but the circumstances of the times did not afford them to continue their education. I graduated high school, attended college, and went to graduate school (not bad for a poor Mississippi boy growing up in the racially torn South). I not only obtained my high school diploma, but in the end, I was to have three colleges degrees. My achievements were all fueled by my unwillingness to duplicate my childhood family experiences. I figured if I obtained what my parents didn't obtain—education, wealth, etc. I'd be a better person. I wouldn't be like my father, but I was wrong. I was the sum total of my past experiences. Deep down inside, I still remembered the painful childhood I had! I remembered the sorrow and hurt on my mother's face, brought about by the traumatic experiences she endured for the sake of her kids. Moreover, I would weep. My soul was scarred! No matter how hard I tried, I still was, inside, that person that I dreaded being!

The question was, How was I to become a better person?—for I needed to be a better person for myself and for those that were in relationship with me. My soul needed healing! I kept the pain inside for so long, hiding it but all the while using it as fuel to propel myself forward. It was killing me! And eventually, what was inside would begin to show itself to those I loved.

After I got married, I became a replica of my father. The same behavior my father demonstrated, I began to demonstrate! My wife became emotionally, a replica of my mother and she was miserable! At some point, I realized that what I was seeing on the outside was a good indication of what was going on in the inside. My soul, my emotional health had deteriorated to a point where it began affecting others. Out of love for my wife, my family, and myself, I realized that I had to get a grip. I realized that I had to seek to restore harmony within my life. And in order to accomplish that, I knew I had to face the demons of my past. I knew I had to overcome them, accept what they had done in my life, no matter how painful, and begin to move towards being a better husband, a better father, a better me.

As I looked back at my past, I realized that I was repeating what my father had demonstrated during my childhood. I accepted the damage as something already, but now no longer having the power to impact my life, and I resolved to use it to effectuate positive change within my life. I knew it was not going to be easy but I knew it had to happen. If there was any hope of breaking the chains of my past and moving on to my future, I had to be reconciled to my past.

To be reconciled to the pain of our past merely means to face it as unpleasant as it was. We must face it if we are to ever move on; if we are ever achieve wholeness and true happiness. Our emotional state, and perhaps our physical state, is beginning to show signs of a system that has been imbalanced for years. Our soul is unhappy, and as a result, it is beginning to show itself. We must work to bring about harmony to our emotional state so that we might live happy, prosperous, healthy, and whole lives. We must find a way to be reconciled to the very thing that has been working to destroy us over the years. We must overcome the fear and devastation of the past, and in order to do this, reconciliation must take place. If you can't find a way to do this within yourself, remember you do not have to go it alone. There are a number of groups, psychologist, psychotherapists, counselors all trained, willing, and waiting to assist you in confronting the pains of your past. All you need to do, is take the first step in deciding you need to do this, and then give one of them a call! It is essential!

Here's a bit of additional advice. You've heard that love covers a multitude of sin. Well, love is a powerful overcomer of pain, trauma, and resistance to change; no matter how deep the pain! No matter how much that person or persons hurt you! You must find love within yourself. You must find that God-given love that is a grace to overcome! Perfect love drives out all fear! If you find yourself yielding again to the stifling pains of past events, look for love within to overcome the situation. Perhaps it may help to consider that the individual that hurt you is God's creation as well. Perhaps it might help to consider that the person that hurt you is someone's child. Perhaps it might help to consider that by chance, their childhood may have been filled with atrocity, and as a result, they are merely repeating the hurt and pain that they experienced at a young age. I know it doesn't seem fair, but it will help you bring out the love for humanity that we all have within.

There is a concept within the field of counseling that is termed, "wounded healer". The concept applies to any individual who has experience some hurt or pain and has learned to find healing through helping others. Within this concept lies an underlying love for humanity. Within this concept, a sacred wisdom reveals that healing comes through helping others. Healing comes through expressing and sharing a reconciled event with others, so that they can begin the road towards healing, and so that you can move down the road of healing as well.

The bible says that Jesus was "wounded for our transgressions, bruised for our iniquities, the chastisement of our peace was

The Plight of the African-American Male

upon him and by His stripes, we were healed". This historical text is a living and breathing organism for those who choose to believe. This is the greatest example of the concept of wounded healer that one can ever search out. One Divine Man, working through the power of the Holy Ghost, to yield one ultimate sacrifice, so that others may be healed and reconciled into eternal life. This is the greatest exploit ever historically or futuristically, that can ever be done to heal the broken hearted and wounded souls.

We, like Christ, must be willing to act in love in order to embrace the unpleasant pains of our past and overcome them! In so doing, we not only recognize that the events of the past shape who we are today, but the experience itself can serve as an impetus that will drive us and those associated with us towards achieving wholeness. It will be a principle by which, if employed continually to daily life, change can result and happiness can be obtained.

Can you imagine if we all reconciled to the pain of our past? What would the world be like? What would our kids look like? I have to believe it will be a better place, for all of the brokenness that plagues so many would be under control. The pains of our past will no longer be concealed causing emotional, physical, and psychological damage to us. No longer will the repressed events of our past be acted out on those that we love. Did you know that if you want to see the harmful effects of adults, who have lived through traumatic childhoods and subsequently become fathers, have on society? All you have to do is look at current census data. If you did, you would see these alarming facts: Fatherless homes account for 63% of youth suicides, 90% are homeless/runaway children, 85% of children have behavior problems, 71% are high school dropouts, 85% of youths are in prison, and well over 50% are teen mothers. More recently, the teenage pregnancy rate has risen, and is currently at a rate higher than it has been over the last ten years.

I believe that at the root cause of these alarming statistics is an adult who never dealt with his childhood, and as a result, never matured to the point where they could be a loving, nurturing, caring, providing, protecting, and emotionally present father, one who makes a visible difference in the lives of his children. The fathers have to be present and active in the lives of the children, in order to change these statistics! The fathers not only have to be present, but they have to be whole. They must be reconciled to the pain of their past, in order to position themselves to stop the vicious cycle that leads to the downfall of their youth, and to the downfall of society as a whole.

Not only do we see the effects of wounded fathers through the statistics of our youth, but we can see the impact through the number of men in prison today, especially the number of African-American men. African American men make up twenty-five percent of those that commit crimes, and seventy-five percent of them are convicted and are subsequently imprisoned, while African American's represent only twelve percent of the United States population! There is something desperately wrong with these figures at large and the incarceration figures in particular! I understand that the system is not favorable towards minorities. But, I also understand as well that not everyone imprisoned is innocent. Most have acted out behavior that caused them to end up in prison.

I have heard of the stories from countless men, who say that they felt they had no choice but to behave in a criminal manner. I have heard the stories of the men who say that their father's were criminals, or they didn't know their father's, as their father's died when they were toddlers either because they were murdered, contracted AIDS or their father's whereabouts

The Plight of the African-American Male

were unknown to them or their mothers. These stories all reek of devastation. They reek of a painful past that have gone unreconciled, and the time has come that we begin the road to healing. We must embrace change if we are to ever fulfill our God-given destiny upon the earth. The entireworld is waiting for the hurt, bruised, battered, and disenfranchised to embrace change, recall, reconcile their past in order for love to abide.

Release

The politico-judicio-educational system in America is no friend of the African American male. As I mentioned earlier, African American men make up the majority of those convicted of crimes and those imprisoned. Additionally, almost 20% of African American men between the ages of 16 to 29 years of age are unemployed, compared to 7.9% of white men of the same age group. 10.1% of African American men between the ages of 18 to 29 years of age are in prison, compared to 1.5% of white men of the same age group. Only 7.5% of African American men between the ages of 18 to 29 graduate from college, compared to 17.3% of their white counterparts of the same age group. (Census Bureau; Current Population Survey Table, accessed online, July 2006) The system has done an atrocious job on the African American male.

I view these figures as indicators of the emotional state of African Americans in general, and African American males in particular. At work within a system that functions to exclude, undermine and eliminate the African American contribution to society, is an undercurrent of emotional instability. How can one be emotionally healthy, when decade in and decade out, generation in and generation out, they see so many talented and gifted men being eaten up in the system? It is not that these men choose to be eaten up but the system is designed to eat them up, and only through an awareness of the system and careful navigation through it, can one hope to escape it.

Bottled up within the souls of the African American male is anger and frustration! They are angry because the system is unfair! They are angry because the system is against them, and does not give them equal opportunity to succeed! They are frustrated because, they play by the rules, but the rules were subject to change unannounced, and all the while, the game is still being played! This is what the African American male is exposed to constantly! Politicians try to trivialize it, but the fact that this is what African American males are experiencing shows up in bureau statistics. Many African American males are killing one another! Black on black crime is on the rise! Suicides among African Americans are on the rise, all the while, the image of African Americans is continuing to erode.

Turn on the television, and the image of the African American male you see is one that is unintelligent and not well spoken. Flip to another channel, and the image portrayed of the African American male is one who is a drug dealer, or one that is portraying him as a violent criminal! Try to escape the media by going to the movies, and you see more of the same! African Americans are bombarded by negative images, and those images are working as part of a larger system to destabilize, dehumanize and denigrate people of African American descent. The result to date is a people who are in need of emotional healing; perhaps total healing.

I believe that a vital part of the process to acquiring healing is releasing. We must release ourselves from the grips of the oppressive system that is bent on keeping us down and tiring us out. The release has to be done emotionally first, and then as we continue to work towards achieving real equality in this society, we will break from the system that works tirelessly to trap us.

Releasing means refusing to allow the system to get you down. It means never telling yourself "no", when the system is trying to get you to give up! You must always keep in mind that you are a part of a greater cause, a greater movement! I talked earlier in this book about how the African American heritage is one that places the male at the center of his family, and as a major positive contributor to his community. We must not forget this, as we encounter opposition to our struggle to be restored to our rightful place within society. We must be determined and disciplined, working to achieve greater, not just for ourselves, but for the greater community. We must not forget the sacrificial spirit of those who came before us.

In order for greater achievement, we must not be hindered by the pains and misfortunes of our past. We must use them as a catalyst for change. We must remember and be reconciled to the pain of our past, but we must release the pain to God for He alone is able to handle our weight and burdens that we may be currently experiencing and the weight and burdens of those that came before us. There is healing in releasing the pain of your past. One cannot run forward speedily nor efficiently or effectively if he/she is carrying additional weight. The weight must be shed in order for them to proceed in a manner that maximizes their strengths and showcases their talents.

While suffering and dying on the cross, Jesus said of his persecutors, "Father, forgive them, for they know not what they do" (Luke 23:34, KJV) In this text, Jesus is suffering and laying down His life for something that He did not do. His life was a propitiation for our sins. Yet, in its climatic moment of sacrifice, Jesus cries out to His father in heaven and asks for forgiveness for those who are carrying out the dreadful deed! Jesus releases the acts of the people exercised on Him and towards Him, and proceeds to continue along His destiny.

I believe that the message being sent and the lesson being taught by Jesus during this great moment of sacrifice is the principle of releasing. We must release individuals from the acts that they have exercised towards us, no matter how devastating. Slavery was a travesty! Racism and discrimination is unjust! Systematic oppression is burdening, but we must release it all unto our Father in heaven, if we are to continue on along the destiny that God has for us! God has hopes and plans for us and we are expected to achieve them. We must not allow anything to keep us from achieving our destiny! We, therefore, must release anything that can hinder us, so that we might run on freely and with liberty.

Releasing has therapeutic benefits. We must release individual(s) from the acts that they have exercised towards us, not for them, but for ourselves. If we do not release them; we give them power over us. The acts that they exercised towards us will continue to plague us, slowly weighing us down until we come to a halt. We must release the burdens for ourselves and not just for them. We cannot give control to anyone and anything other than almighty God. Jesus is Lord and Him only, and if we work under His lordship, we are free to move forward and bring about change in our lives and the lives of our families and communities. Change is facilitated by releasing the burdens of your past and forgiving those who have hurt you. Releasing will free you to run forward and accomplish the things that God has created you to accomplish. It is important to release for ourselves, as well as forgiving those who hurt us.

Educate to Integrate not Assimilate

Education is empowering and can be a powerful means of empowering the disempowered and disenfranchised. It can be an indispensable weapon that can be used to fight against and overcome racism and discrimination. Education is a powerful force that can be used to turn around the devastation and socio-economic disparity seen in the African American families and their communities. Education is power and the key to turning around socio-economic disparity in our communities and to re-instituting the African male into his central role in the family and community.

Education must be undertaken with the understanding that we must educate to successfully integrate into society—to become an integral part of it. We must use education as a platform from which our gifts and talents can be launched and used for the betterment of society. We must be use education wisely that we might integrate into society and not merely assimilate to the norms of society, for assimilation merely smothers our gifts and talents. It causes us to loose our identities, and not to use our very uniqueness and diversity to broader the horizons and hopes of this world. We therefore must be careful to educate, to integrate, and not assimilate.

Looking closer at education and the method of educating, I have come to realize that very little thought has been given to the method of education that one undergoes. From early childhood to adulthood, what we have been exposed to, what we have overheard, and what we have been taught institutionally has shaped who we are. The method of exposure or learning undoubtedly has contributed much to our learning capabilities, and as such, has shaped the way we learn. Considering this, it would be safe to conclude that the systems in which we have acquired education can either mold an individual in the way of oppression (in a way that does not give the individual the opportunity to use his/her unique gifts and talents), or position an individual towards liberation. In either case, the power of education is expressed and the method in which it is introduced can become the catalyst for change or assimilation. I'd like to share as a means of re-enforcing and bringing clarity to my point, my attitude and experience with education.

The bible says that a friend is born out of adversity. Throughout my life, I have been constantly challenged by adversity, and through it friendships were born. One friend of which I speak is education, and the mother of it has been oppressive social injustice of the rural south.

Having grown up in rural Mississippi in the sixties, I am no stranger to adversity. Hangings of colored people either for sport or because they were rebels to the status quo, was a mainstay in Mississippi during this time. Invisible lines of demarcation traversed the geography. If you were colored, you knew your place. Regardless of age, every white person was to be referred to as "Yes Sir" or "Yes Ma'am," depending upon the gender of course. The entire landscape of the South was painted with oppression; everything was either black or white, no gray. If you were white, you were right, wealthy, intelligent, and privileged. The entire world belonged to you. If you were black (or in the vernacular of the time, colored) you were the lowest of the lowest. You were incapable of learning. You were the ethnos, the other ones, and were not to mix with the esteemed social class of the time.

As one might imagine, an environment such as the one previously depicted was one swollen with tension, even the air that a colored person breathed seemed to be rationed. Something had to change if we were to go on living. We could no longer be ignored. The efforts of Malcolm X, Martin Luther King, and the likes, demanded that the oppressive discriminatory practices so prevalent in the rural south could no longer be ignored. Some of the offspring of attempts to stabilize and neutralize the south were integration and bussing.

I was totally adjusted in my classroom. The environment was very comfortable. I had colored teachers. There were colored students. I had colored friends. My environment was a utopia. Then one day we are all separated, bussed in a manner that was reminiscent of the transatlantic slave trade, to an all white institution twenty miles in the opposite direction of where I was accustomed. Thoughts ravished my mind: "What did we do wrong?"; "Why did I have to leave my friends?" etc. We were thrust right into the middle of chaos. The white students didn't want us there and we didn't want to be there. Interracial fighting became the norm. We were in the midst of integration and it wasn't going smoothly. Day after day, the occurrences were the same and there was no hope of any change. We were there to stay, so we had better make the best of it. I settled in and began to focus intently on my studies, ignoring all that was around me. Integration and bussing had taught me to accept that which I seemingly had no power to control. A lesson that in some way, shape, or form remains with me over forty years later. Adversity was beginning to have labor pains.

I remained in my one-dimensional, educational, mental tunnel all through high school. I had learned that regardless of what was going on around me, the task still needed to be completed. As a result, I performed well academically. I was able to spew out exactly what my teachers wanted me to. I had become a recorder, able to play back all that I had heard because of the unwillingness to think critically. In fact, I was also afraid, believing that chaos would ensue again if I challenged the status quo.

I graduated in the top ten of my class in an all predominately white institution. At graduation, I heard all of the white students, practically all below me academically, being announced as having received scholarships to this college or to that college. I became confused. I questioned what was going on (in my mind of course). I had better grades. Why wasn't I offered academic scholarships to any colleges? I soon discovered that the school guidance counselor had not counseled me at all. I was left to go it alone. I was number thirteen of fifteen kids, and none before me had ever attended college. I had no road map, no blueprint to follow. I had to do it myself. I couldn't trust anyone to help me. I was being educated to go it alone. Adversity's contractions were getting stronger.

After high school graduation, I took some time to reflect. I looked back over my life, considering all that I had been exposed to and had overcome. I looked at my brothers' and my sisters' consideration of choices they had made regarding life. I looked at my family as a whole and assessed that, although we were not very well educated, we were a very talented family. Nevertheless, we remained in poverty. I looked at my white counterparts drawing upon their academic efforts while in high school, and quickly discerned that I saw no difference between them and us (besides skin color). I recognized that college was not an option for them. It was mandatory. It was then that I began to experience fear, a new type of fear. This fear was the fear of remaining in poverty, constantly being victimized by the oppressive discriminatory practices of the rural south. I realized that I had to do something different. Devoid of a blueprint, I reached for that which seemed obvious. I would attempt to mirror the steps of my white counterparts. I was to assimilate.

I enrolled in a ninety-seven percent white college. I was to dress the part (as best as I could afford). I was to speak their language. I was to be seen as non-threatening in an attempt to penetrate their civic organizations. I was to be all that they required of me and I succeeded (so I thought). It wasn't until I was about to graduate that I began to realize that assimilation was not only uncomfortable to me, but it represented betrayal to all that had labored before me. The goal of those that had paved the way for the black race was for us to contribute to bettering our race as a whole, not to lose sight of and dishonor it by assimilating.

These reflections took on life for me when one of my professors informed me that she was going to change one of my grades from a B to an A, for seemingly no reason at all. I began to think that if she was going to do that now, how many times will she do it in the negative direction throughout my stay at the university. I had another similar incident when my advisor (of the white race) attempted very strongly to get me to reconsider my plans to go to an all black college to pursue graduate work. His reasoning, although he assured me that he was looking out for my best interest, appeared to me as though he had a problem with Historically Black Institutions. I quickly realized that assimilation had not liberated me. I was still trapped below the hull of oppression and discrimination. Again, I was facing adversity and her contractions were getting intense.

I had achieved a milestone for my family. I was the first to graduate from college. Unsure of what I was going to do with the degree I obtained, I decided to work during the summer on the farm with my dad. It was this experience that was to throw me for a total loop. We were assigned (my dad and I and a few others) to spray all of the cotton plants in the fields with pesticide in order to rid the crop of weeds. After working for some time, we were out of pesticide and decided and to take the long walk back to the shop where we were to ask the supervisor (a white man) to refuel our vessels. However, when we got there he was nowhere to be found. In an attempt to remedy the situation, I walked over to the bottle of concentrated pesticide, read the directions for dilution, and proceeded to dilute the product. It was then that screams bombarded my ears. Stop!!!! Don't do it! Startled, I froze and looked at my father and the other workers with amazement. My amazement quickly turned to disgust, and I realized that the only way to get out of this oppression was through education. I had to totally thrust myself into education in an attempt to liberate my family from this oppressive regime. A friend had been birthed through adversity and that friend was education.

Indeed a friend is born out of adversity. Adversity in my life had become the stimulus through which I was to achieve liberation for my family. No longer were we to be victims of the oppressive discriminatory regime of the rural south. Education was to be the tool through which we were to escape poverty. Education was to be the weapon that we were to use to destroy the victimization brought about through discrimination and social injustice. Adversity had indeed shaped the way I lived my life. It had shaped the way I viewed every situation.

Adversity had birthed in me the desire to acquire knowledge. I was to approach education with an attitude that no one was going to help me achieve anything. I had to do it alone. I was to block out all distractions around me and focus on the task at hand, while at the same time maintaining my ethnicity and my identity that had been shaped by my black experience. Liberation had screamed without the chained doors of adversity, and I embraced education as my friend.

Education has allowed me to contribute to my family and to my community. The experiences that I have gained over the years, I have shared with them, and as a result, many who might not have attended college or gained further education have done so. Education has raised the socio-economic level of my family from below poverty level to above it, and all that have tasted the fruit of it have maintained their identities and have contributed to those who have come behind them. Our communities are on the rise. It is a work in progress, and I believe that as we continue to educate we will reach great heights as a people and as a nation. We will re-establish our family ties to the point of old, and we will rebuild our communities so that they may flourish the way God had intended them. They will be safe havens to all who choose to come within their borders, and will owe it all to education, which is the great equalizer and friend to all who choose to embrace it.

Restoration

Education is paramount to positioning the African American to be restored to his place within his family and within his community. However, empowerment through education is still one step in the process. We must work to bring about a fundamental change in the way the African American male views and participates within the family unit.

As I have previously delineated, slavery, as well as the current governmental system of today, has done an atrocious job on the African American Male. He has been excluded from positive contribution to society, as well as from positively contributing to his family and community. This has been the case for generations. Not only will raising the economic and social level of the African American male be enough to restore our families and communities, but there is a need for work to be done on his psyche.

Sixty percent of African American families are fatherless and for the remaining forty percent that are not, many of the fathers are present in body only, and are not actively engaged in the rearing of their children or the affirmation and nurturing of their spouse. Edwin Louis Cole makes the following statement regarding the fathers of today: "Today, instead of the absentee father being the curse of our day, it is 'fatherlessness.' The difference is that rather than being absent from the family, there is an absence of concern for the family. Fatherlessness is the curse of our day."

We must work to change the psyche of the African American male, in a way that regains the attitudes that his forefathers demonstrated towards their children and family. Programs must be put in place that re-teach the African American male what his role is within his family, and how to carry out that role. The African American male has to be re-taught what it means to be a man, a father, and to be a husband. The African American male must be taught in hopes of gaining an understanding the impact of his presence, position and paternal values. This must be done in order for our families to achieve wholeness, as well as restore a positive image and vitality of the male within his family and community.

The programs needed to transform the attitudes of the African American male are critical to the success of our communities. The African American male must be taught the history of his role within the family and community. He must be taught in a manner that underscores the need for him to regain his rightful place within his family and community, for in so doing, it will be therapeutic for him as well as for his community. Edwin H. Friedman puts it this way: "…not only does our position in our extended families affect how we function in other relationships, but also the efforts to gain better differentiation of self in that extended field will have corresponding effects at home, at work, and on our health. The more we can understand our own origins, the more we can sympathize with theirs; the more we can define our own families, the more we can help them modify the influence of, or mobilize the strengths in, theirs. And the more we realize how difficult it can be to gain any measure of self-differentiation, the more humbly we can appreciate their plight."

Edwin H. Friedman delineates the need to understand our origins. He underscores the the interrelatedness of an individual and his family and community; how they need each other to survive. It is the lack of this interrelatedness within the African American communities that have caused them to deteriorate, and the people to lack focus and drive. Restoration of the transformed, mentally and socially adjusted African American male to his role within family and community, will initiate a revolution within it and will serve to promote emotional health and decrease fragmentation.

As you can see, real change is need for, in the words of Margaret Kornfeld when speaking on first order change (personal change) versus second order change (change that effects a group): "When people make a first order change, they do so within their present system or circumstance. With a second order change, they change the system, or circumstance itself." (Margaret Kornfeld) In first order change people, adjust to their present situation. They learn to function better but their present situation does not change. A second order change is a paradigmatic shift in which a whole constellation of beliefs, attitudes, and actions are altered because of a new perception of reality. In second order change, a whole system is changed. African Americans in general and African American men in particular are in need of second order change. We must be transformed in a way that not only benefits ourselves, but in a way that benefits society.

It is critical that the approach used to restore the African American male to his family and community be done in a manner that celebrates his value and does not ostracize him for past failures. We must seek to restore him in a manner that is reflective of our love and deep concern for his well being, and demonstrate that we are ecstatic because of his return. We must be careful not to attack or appear defensive of our homes. We must be open and willing to dedicate ourselves to a journey that will be mutually beneficial, no matter how rough the journey may be in the beginning.

In addition to our being open and receptive of the African American male's return to his family, it will be even more important for the African American male to be open and remain open to the change that is occurring in his life. He must be open to returning home and to his community again. It is critical that he sees his value within the family and within his community. He must understand that he has something to contribute to the well-being of the family and community, and therefore, present himself with the confidence that he will make a difference. An embracing of who he is and what he has to offer, as well as an understanding of the dynamics of the family and community and how he can contribute, will be most important to his restoration. Monica McGoldrick, renowned family therapist, states regarding the family wholeness: "The fundamental guideline for going home again is: Don't attack and don't defend. Going home again means finding a way to be yourself and stay connected to your family without defending yourself or attacking others. The typical dysfunctional roles people get into in their families—in which one becomes the caretaker and the other the caretakee or one always pursues and the other distances—develop because family members have not evolved sufficient sense of self to function for themselves."

As we have delineated earlier, the root cause of destructive behavior exhibited by the African American male lies within family function. Moreover, it is steeped in his world-view perception and definition of family. His family is not only his immediate family, but encompasses his entire community, and is shaped by a need to contribute to community. Restoration, therefore, must begin here with the family. However, at the very center of the African American culture is the church. Traditionally, the African American is very spiritual. Their hope is to live a life that is pleasing and mindful of a higher calling. The church is a family member to the African American. God is the head of the family and the community. God is their source, and without Him they cannot do anything. It is therefore most important that the church have a direct role in restoring the African American male to his central role within the family and community. The church must be actively engaged in the process. The messages delivered by the church must be relevant, empowering and liberating. They must be authentic and reflective of a prophetic word that restores, regenerates, and rebuilds the soul, character, and mind of the African American male.

The church must be willing, ready and able to take direct action from a social justice perspective, in order to right the wrongs of injustice that plague the African American community in particular and minorities at large. The church must be involved in social justice, else the preaching, teaching, shouting and praising will be less than authentic. They must be directly involved in letting their voice be heard within the halls of justice without fear of retaliation. The church must represent and take on a sacrificial role just as Christ did, if the hopes of a new community will ever be realized.

J. Philip Wogaman articulated this most succinctly when he said "Christian thought devoid of action is inauthentic;" and Martin Luther King in his letter from the Birmingham jail, articulated the need for the church to be engaged in direct action without fear of retaliation when he said: "We who engage in nonviolent direct action are not the creators of tension. We merely bring to the surface the hidden tension that is already alive." Martin understood that the church holds a powerful position within the African American community, and its involvement must be solicited if true change is to be realized within it. The church must be willing, ready, able and authentic in its involvement in revitalizing, healing and restoration of the African American male to his family and community.

Are today's Mega-Churches Effective in Liberating the African American Male and Restoring Him into our Families & Communities?

There is much devastation that has impacted the African American family and community. Because of socio-economic disparity and systematic exclusion, the family and the African American male that are central to their vitality have become dysfunctional. The African American male is accustomed to being head of his home and a positive contributor to his community. However, the destructive forces that have attacked our families and communities have left him searching.

For the African American family and communities, the survival force that allows them to keep pressing and to "keep on keeping on" is their spiritual foundation. Their belief in God has enabled them to cope with the devastation of slavery and racial discrimination. However, the traditional African American family is beginning to move along the path of extinction. The spirituality that our grandparents and great-grandparents demonstrated seems to be lessening. While church attendance is not diminishing significantly, the fruits of spiritual living do not seem to be manifesting themselves as of old. I therefore ask the question, are today's churches effective? The churches are larger now—mega—now! Our churches have thousands of members! They are growing quantitatively, but due to the breakdown in family and in our communities, I'm wondering if they are growing qualitatively.

Whatever happened to the small, cozy church where every member of the church not only knew each other, but also knew each other's families? Where now is the small, intimate church where the pastor pays a visit to each family throughout the week, and then closes out the week with a Sunday dinner at "Aunt Bessies"? Are the days fading away when the church was not only the center for religious experience and growth within the individual households, but a place that connected, nurtured, and directed the very community?

Do you remember the saying: "It takes a village to raise a child"? Well, there was a time when one could substitute the word "village" with the word "church", and the saying would carry the same, if not more, meaning. The church was the driving force for the community and the driving force for the family. One could count on the church to rear our children in a manner that helped ensure their success within this unfair and sometimes treacherous world. One could count on the church to be a father to the fatherless, a husband to the widow, food for the hungry, and a shelter for the homeless. One could count on the church to mature each individual in such a way that whatever or whenever something seemed to get off track in our lives, we knew that we could always count on Jesus to get us through. We could count on the church to provide correct guidance.

Well, just as we were once kids and now are adults, and just as there were manual typewriters then electric typewriters and now computers, change must occur. With this change has come a shift not only in technology, but a shift in the church as well. The church as we once knew it seems to be slowly fading away, and as it does, rising out of its demise is the next version of the church. A paradigm shift is occurring and out of this shift has emerged the now prevalent "mega" churches of today.

There is an affinity that today's age has for the "mega" church. C. S. Clark states in "Religion in America" 1994, that "Pentecostal and conservative Protestant faiths have grown by over 300% and 200% respectively since 1950." But what is it that draws so many people to these churches? What is it that makes these churches grow at such an alarming rate?

Upon careful examination of these churches, one finds that most, if not all of these churches, offer a myriad of programs and services. Day care services are offered. Pre Kindergarten through eighth grade schooling is offered in some of these "mega" churches. Practical living classes are offered in some of these churches. There are programs in media, drama, dance, etc. Perhaps this is what draws the masses to these churches. K. H. Sargeant in a Masters Thesis entitled "Marketing the Church" University of Virginia, Charlottesville, VA 1994 exclaims, "people switch churches based on stylistic qualities of churches like better children's programs, more entertainment, and the commitment to reach seekers". But these services can be found in abundance outside of the church, so what is it really that draws such a large number of people into one location, so much that the "mega" church is birthed. Could it be dynamic Pentecostal preaching with messages that focus heavily on prosperity rather than the doctrine of the church, could be the source of this growth? I believe so. We hear it on church networks. If we attend any one of these churches, we are gripped by one of these sermons and stirred up by emotional displays of the gospel heralded.

I must admit this is most exhilarating and gripping, but what is the end result of this emotionalism and hopes of prosperity?

In the end, are the people who join these churches spiritually edified, or are they fueled for a brief moment and run out of gas once they leave the service? Are these people being developed into spiritual maturity? We will begin to examine these as well as other concerns as we take a closer look at the "mega" church.

History and Demographic of Church

As was cited earlier, Pentecostal and Protestant Faith Churches have grown some 300 and 200 percent respectively since 1950. On the other hand, traditional churches are reported to be on the decline. This is phenomenal growth for the Pentecostal and Protestant Faith Churches. With this growth, however, is the church upholding its responsibility to develop its congregants to spiritual maturity, or is it merely focusing all of its energies and talents on the quantitative growth of the church? If the latter is the case, the church by default is oppressing the ones it once sought to liberate.

Let us begin to examine further a once small community church that has grown throughout the years into one of the largest churches in the Northeast, in hopes of obtaining some answers to our questions. The Cathedral International, once the historical Second Baptist Church, began its rise to prominence in 1983 with 125 members, and now boasts well over 7,000 members. The church functions as one church in three locations providing spiritual guidance and development for three major urban areas within New Jersey: Perth Amboy, Plainfield, and Asbury Park. These areas have experienced major revitalization since the emergence of the Cathedral International into their respective communities. Headed by one God fearing, holiness preacher and one dynamic, discerning, administrative genius preacher/teacher, this church has been not only a revitalizing force for the communities in which they are present, but is a model for churches on the road to "mega" church status.

The Cathedral International, over the last several years, experienced phenomenal growth financially, spiritually, and quantitatively. The church continues to grow financially boasting projected revenue well over 6 million annually and the church is expanding to a fourth location in the near future having recently purchased 100 acres of land in the surrounding area.

The church is a multi-cultural, multi-ethnicity church with emphasis on holiness, restoration of family, prosperity, and spiritual development. The church is intent on Evangelizing, Educating, Emancipating, and Empowering individuals within the community at large. The church focuses it energies and talents on Lifting and Liberating humanity to the point of reverence for the Most High God, and in a way that reflects in each individual's daily life. However, could it be possible that this model church with over 65 relevant ministries and excellent administrative infrastructure, be failing in its efforts to develop individuals into spiritual maturity? Is it possible that some individuals could be slipping through the cracks and not be receiving the necessary spiritual impartation that breaks the yoke of bondage and sets the oppressed free? Let us take a closer look by examining a case study developed around one of the sixty-five ministries that the Cathedral hosts.

Case Study:

Focus:

This case study will begin to examine the perspective of the now prevalent "mega churches" who demonstrate Pentecostal fervor with an emphasis on prosperity, in order to enhance quantitative growth. By placing emphasis on quantitative growth (numerical growth), leaving spiritual growth (qualitative growth) to chance, the church, by default, has oppressed those of whom it once sought to liberate.

Background:

The Cathedral International is a historical Baptist Church located in Perth Amboy, New Jersey that by creed acknowledges that they are Baptist by denomination, Pentecostal by experience and Holiness by choice. The Cathedral International has experienced phenomenal growth. In its infancy, it was a church of 125 members, but now boasts membership in excess of 7,000, all under the auspices of one dynamic Baptist, Pentecostal, and Holiness Bishop who has a sincere love for God. The congregation is approximately 70 % women and 30 % men. Representation from diverse cultures (Caribbean, European, American, and African) is a prized attribute. A number of testimonies are presented weekly that express the realized hope of individuals and families who have been delivered from poverty, alcohol addiction, drug addiction, prostitution, gang violence, etc., and that demonstrates the active fulfillment of the churches four fold mission: to Evangelize, Educate, Emancipate, and Empower through Loving, Lifting, and Liberating Humanity.

The Cathedral International has revitalized a number of underdeveloped urban communities through its structure as one church in three locations. The mission of the Bishop to Evangelize, Educate, Emancipate, and Empower is one that resonates throughout all that it touches, and provides meat to an otherwise hungry and impoverished community. The Cathedral International, from my point of view, is the model church; a church of which God is undoubtedly well pleased.

In support of the mission of the church, one of the over 65 ministries that the Cathedral offers is the Men's Ministry. After first participating as a member of the ministry for two years, the opportunity arose for me to provide leadership to the ministry. I was to enter this position using my experience as a once participant, to effectively realize the mission of the church in the lives of the men who chose to undergo this transformation. Men who had chosen to spend every other Saturday morning hearing, digesting, and participating in a ministry that looks to change their diverse meaning of manhood.

The demographics of the Cathedral Men's Ministry from the time of my involvement until now, fluctuates between 15 to 25 men of predominantly African-American descent, most from urban disadvantaged communities, all reflecting generational ills and battle scars from the weight of this world. It is interesting to note that these men represent 1% of the total population of men in the church. Notwithstanding the success of the church, this fact alone raises questions as to the effectiveness of the church in providing ministry that touches, retains, and spiritually matures members of both genders.

Development:

On the first Saturday of which I was to lead the Men's Ministry, approximately fifteen men participated in the ministerial session. My plan was to develop a rather riveting message in true preacher style that would address the need for spiritual maturity. At the end of my emotional, dynamic preaching experience, my inner Spirit beckoned, "now what"? The men sat there communicating to me how prolific of a speaker I was and how "on fire" I was, but I heard and felt no desire for the men to want more of God. I understood that the way change occurs is that you must first resolve within yourself that you are going to identify and then confront that which vexes you. I knew that talking it out amongst your peers was valuable. I even

The Plight of the African-American Male

knew that in order for the men to transform, the focus could not and must not be on me, but how they were to participate in their own transformation. The goal was to promote spiritual maturity amongst the men and to assist in healing, delivering, and shaping the mind, body, and soul of the man. Achieving this goal would be critical to the success of the ministry.

Having left the first meeting feeling as though I had failed in my debut, I labored in prayer concerning the correct approach needed to achieve my and the churches goal. After a week of seeking and reading materials, I decided to introduce a book to the men entitled "Communication, Sex, and Money" by Ed. Coles. I felt that spiritual maturity involved developing closer relationships, and what better way to initiate dialogue around relationships than to discus the three things that have been proven to be most devastating to relationships. This book addressed communication in relationships first from the perspective of God to Mankind, and then equated this to communication between spouse or significant other. The book addressed questions concerning family responsibility, accountability, sensitivity, finances etc. all issues that impacted the men personally. This book set the stage for dialogue.

I facilitated the conversation amongst the men, occasionally sharing personal experiences in hopes of drawing even more information from them in order to further dialogue. In relative quick order, all of the men were actively participating in discussion of the material covered in the first few pages of the book. This open dialogue continued until our scheduled time was up. However, because of this dialogue, so many issues and questions arose that could be and that needed to be addressed in subsequent meetings.

At the end of the sessions no participants including myself, wanted to leave. We felt as though so much had been accomplished. We felt that finally someone had begun to address the real issues facing every day life such as: "my spouse sometimes makes me so mad that I feel like screaming and shouting"; "I've lost intimacy with my wife, how can I get it back?" My father wasn't there to raise me, how can I know how to be a man?" These and many other questions was the subject of our conversations, and was all brought about through engaged pedagogy. It was something that we all could identify with, something that placed us on the same level, the same playing field. It was something that caused us to let down the wall of defense we had learned to raise so high since childhood, that something was to the naked eye a book but the method was engaged pedagogy.

After a terrible beginning, I had searched and prayed for an approach that would lend itself to men taking part in their own spiritual development. An approach that would help begin the road to healing generational ills, and the pain being inflicted by a system that is innately apathetic. I had discovered an approach, that if expanded upon, could help so many men, and if duplicated, could be an answer to family dysfunctionality, gang violence, drug addiction, alcoholism, church phobia, etc.

Later on, when thinking over what had transpired in the ministerial session, I could not help but be concerned with how a church as large and as successful as The Cathedral International could miss addressing the concerns of these men. I thought that if this was the case throughout the church, then how many other Congregationalist were effectively not being ministered to, and as a result, not being assisted in their spiritual development? In assessing the church, I realized that although sixty-plus ministries were in place to deal with the plethora of issues that plagued humankind, there was no system in place in each of the ministries to effectively minister to and develop the spiritual maturity of its membership. Yes, Christian Education Ministry and Discipleship Ministry were alive and functioning, however, the curriculum was not one that engaged its members at each level and challenged them to transcend their preconceived boundaries. I believe that on the grand scale, emotionalism (what I call Pentecostal fervor) and messages surrounding prosperity, holiness, and sanctification merely scratched the surface in the sanctuary, serving to enhance qualitative growth but left most, if not all of the congregation in a stage of underdevelopment. In effect, Pentecostal fervor and promised prosperity messages had, through neglect, oppressed the people of whom it was attempting to liberate, merely shuffling them off to the small corner of a room labeled "Sunday School", in hopes of this ill-equipped program to develop its membership into spiritual maturity.

Critical Pedagogical Issues:

This case study highlights the ineffectiveness of the traditional church structure in developing its membership to spiritual maturity. It highlights a leader who initially was not equipped to handle effectively a group of men who were committed to spiritual transformation. This is underscored by the leader's first attempt at facilitating the ministerial session, defaulting to the traditional "**banking system of education**" (a system of repeating or regurgitation what was lectured) that was learned throughout life. However, through genuine care and concern for the men involved, the leader submitted to prayer and research that ultimately led to a method that proved useful.

Intricate to this case are several concepts of engaged pedagogy. The engaged pedagogical concept of **self-actualization** (the concept of one desiring to become more than he/she is, i.e. the desire to reach then exercise ones fullest potential) is evident in this case study. The leader first, and then the session participants were able to come to a realization of self. The leader, after failing on the first attempt to address the issues of the participants, performed a self assessment and quickly realized that ministry was not about him. It was not how well he could preach or how much deep revelation he could relay, but ministry was about helping, healing, and liberating others, and in the process you are liberated, healed, and helped. The participants after seeing the transformation in the leader, were then able to look deep within themselves and began pulling out and addressing their secret parts, which led to their self actualization.

Theory is another concept exemplified in this case study. All participants including the leader engaged in theory. In order to truly address concerns, critical analysis, self-evaluation, and reflection must first occur. The leader engaged in theory surrounding his failure. The participants engaged in theory with regards to the un-confessed, repressed secrets, along with those things that they failed to or were unwilling to confront. The result was an experience that ultimately led to an equal voice for all involved.

Praxis (theory and practice) was yet another concept inherent to this case study. Theory and practice together was evident in the participants coming to voice. At first, only the leader truly had a voice, but after a change in the teaching approach, all participants came to voice and as such, the stage was set for their and the teacher's transformation.

Lastly, **dialogue** is an engaged pedagogical concept evident in this case study. After much theory and a change in the session teaching dynamics, all of the session participants were able to enter into open discussion concerning the issues that they questioned for so long. Dialogue in an environment that was open, accepting, non-condescending, and loving empowered all involved. All participants felt valued, and as a result, freely shared their thoughts and concerns. Open and honest dialogue assisted everyone in the healing process. Open and honest dialogue helped everyone involved to come to terms with so much that they had repressed for so long, and as a result, they were the better for it. They were on the road to developing into spiritual maturity.

Study Conclusion:

This case study illustrates a valid challenge facing the traditional church. In an era where Pentecostal fervor (emotionalism) and the promise of prosperity dominate the church, quantitative growth has taken precedence over qualitative growth. The offspring of such a disposition are the "mega" churches of today. As a result of the church's disposition, the responsibility of spiritual maturation of the members at large has been left to fester away in the corner of some small room labeled "Sunday School". Spiritual development of the church's membership is left to leaders, who in most cases, are ill equipped to handle the myriad of issues that impact its members. In fact, through unintentional neglect, oppression takes root in the church; slowly nibbling away at its stability until, (unless drastic measures are taken and the church's perspective changed) a rift occurs that is potentially so devastating that the church can no longer thrive.

There is hope however, on some levels engaged pedagogical techniques were employed and have proven successful at fulfilling the church's four-fold mission at the level of its original intent. Dialogue, Praxis, Theory, Self Actualization, etc were concepts utilized (though not bearing this terminology) in order to promote and assist the spiritual development of its participants.

Larry McCullum

Questions for the reader:

1. How might engaged pedagogy concepts be integrated into traditional church practice in order to promote spiritual maturity amongst its members?

2. How might the structure of "mega churches" be modified in a way that maintains quantitative growth while at the same time ensuring qualitative growth?

3. How might a leader devoid of concern and genuine empathy for a ministry in which he/she is involved use this experience to promote self-actualization?

4. How does one evaluate traditional church polity and its impact on promoting spiritual development amongst church membership?

5. Comment on how the dynamics of a church might look if the traditional pulpit preaching/teaching were removed and the general congregation were allowed to come to voice?

As one can see from this case study, it is possible to neglect the needs of some of the members of a "mega" church. I am sure that this statement can be found true for smaller traditional churches also, but the size alone dictates that the number of people not having their issues addressed, and therefore remaining in bondage to these issues, is larger than the size of some traditional churches. Whether by default or neglect, the "mega" church, in some areas, are not equipped to handle the myriad of issues that impact its members. Charles Foster in his book "Educating Congregations", (Nashville: Abington, 1994) page 21, puts it this way: "Churches have not acknowledged the diminishing capacity –even the brokenness—of their education. These churches are no longer capable of building up communities of faith adequate to the contemporary challenge of praising God and serving neighbor for the sake of the emancipatory transformation of the world." Let us examine some of the issues that this case study uncovered in this "mega" church.

Focus Issues:

One of the key focus issues of this case is the lack of self-actualization. One can see from the case study that the group participants had a variety of questions that indicated their lack of self-actualization. They had questions concerning parenting, having come from dysfunctional families themselves. They had questions concerning manhood, being that their fathers were not around. These individuals were beginning to realize that they were not whole, something was missing, and they needed support.

Most important to spiritual maturity is not only reconciliation to Christ, but also reconciliation to self. If a method is not present within the structure of the church that seeks to create wholeness an individual will not grow.

It is well known that most of the individuals in urban predominantly minority churches come from backgrounds that were inhibitory to their emotional and psychological development. That is to say that there is a fragmentation that exists among minority members that is present, due to either having been reared in a dysfunction family or having a traditional family, but not one that nurtured individual development. The end result of such unfortunate circumstances is that these individuals usually present as individuals that have no real concept of self. They do not really know who they are, how they function, and/or how they are supposed to function within the community. These individuals are not self-actualized.

Critical to the self-actualization process is the need to have a pedagogical method that engages not only the participants of a particular session, but the leader as well. There has to exist within the dynamics of the group a feeling of equality and not a feeling of condescension amongst the leader and the members of the group. Every effort must be made to eliminate the lingering effects of the banking system at work in education and society at large. Every individual must be made to feel and believe that they matter, and what they have to say is valuable to the group as a whole.

As an aid to self-actualization, the leader must implement a model that promotes critical thinking and self-analysis. Perhaps the Winks Model detailed in "Transforming Bible Study" (Nashville: Abingdon Press, 1980) might prove useful. The leader must engage the participants as well as himself in a series of questions that seek to provoke the group members to do introspection. With each question, the group participants learn a little more about who they are, what their likes and dislikes are, what upsets them, what makes them happy, etc. Each question serves to bring to the surface the inner person. Once this process is implemented and continued, it won't be long before each group participant, the leader included, find themselves in a brand new world, aware of themselves and their potential contributions to it. These individuals would have migrated from the expression of several identities, of which none were real to them, to a place where they are sure of who they are and what their purpose is in the community as a whole. These individuals would have been self-actualized.

Another key focus issue of this case study is dialogue. As one can see from the case, the church leader began to facilitate the group session initially, utilizing the banking system method evidently taught him throughout life. The act of speaking to, and in some case down to, participants did not offer much value to the development of the spiritual maturity of this group. In order to develop, individuals must be allowed to think critical. They must be allowed to perform higher order thinking so that they will be able to make sound decisions based on careful analysis of a situation.

Modifying the room dynamics in such a way that facilitates dialogue is critical to self- development. Individuals must be positioned in a manner that facilitates free exchange of information. They must be encouraged to speak and made to feel as though they have equal voice. No one person is greater than the other. Free, uninhibited exchange of information increases self-value and self-esteem. Individuals begin to hear themselves, and others and begin to think critically prior to speaking, as well as to think critically about what others are saying. Individuals in this type of group dynamic reflect theologically about biblical issues and how they affect their lives as well as society, and as a result, the ground for spiritual development is being cultivated.

It is through dialogue that an individual learns about himself and about others. Dialogue is critical for development and growth, and the absence of it will only result in perpetuation of the status quo, and along with it, the ills that continue to plague society. If the community is to grow in a manner that is healthy for all, dialogue must occur, and the spiritual maturation that will result will help promote a healthy church environment and a better community as a whole.

The final critical issue that will be addressed is Praxis, the application of theory and practice. What would it benefit if dialogue is all that occurs and no action is ever put to dialogue?

No doubt, we will be as the Apostle Paul puts it in 1 Corinthian 13:1 "...as sounding brass, or a tinkling cymbal" (King James Version). The concern with traditional church settings is that there is preaching but no follow-up on the results of what was preached. How does one continue or why does one continue to speak if his/her words have no effect? The ultimate goal is to facilitate change within an individual's life. You want the individual to grow.

Preaching is not about the preacher. It is about the individuals preached to. So often prevalent in small study groups or in Sunday Schools of the church, is a lay minister or lay person who is not adequately trained to handle the myriad of issues of which he/she is confronted. The modus operandi is usually aimed at giving the individual time to hone his/her preaching skill, and never solely for the development of the individuals of those that attend sessions led by these individuals. I know that individuals called into ministry must receive practical training, but must it be at the expense of those that are diligently seeking to develop spiritually? A method must be developed that addresses the needs of those seeking to be trained for ministry, as well as to address the needs of those looking for spiritual development.

Notwithstanding the issue of ministering practical training and its impact on the spiritual maturity of its participants, the absence of a curriculum that properly addresses the spiritual development and the myriad of issues of those attending bible classes or Sunday school needs attention, if at all possible. Charles Foster in "Educating Congregations" (Nashville: Abington, 1994, pp 28) makes this argument: "Curriculum resources cannot be written to respond to the range of personal or group concerns or expectations." If Foster is correct, then what is the means for adequately addressing the needs of the congregation? Are we to proceed with the understanding that some individuals will never reach their full potential? I am not so sure that Foster is entirely correct when he makes this statement. The curriculum of the educational ministries of the church must reflect diversity, while at the same time address the personal needs of the individuals of which the ministries seek to serve. The curriculum cannot be just theoretical devices that can never be used as an effective tool to bring about spiritual transformation. They must be developed to bring about this cause.

The questions posed throughout this essay as well as the case study embedded within, reveal critical concerns facing the church population and the world with the surgence of the "mega" church. And although these churches meet the service needs of their congregations, they quite possibly could be falling short on the qualitative needs of these very same members. As churches grow large in number and as the leaders of these churches work to sustain such phenomenal growth, a myriad of issues arise that impact the life of the church and the community at large. Unless measures are taken to address these issues, the result perhaps may be a rift so devastating that the church can no longer thrive.

Assessment of one of these "mega" churches revealed concerns as to the educational structure that exists within the church. It is the educational ministry that has been tasked with ensuring that the preached word is cultivated in the lives of the congregation. This cultivation is usually relegated to small group bible study and/or Sunday school instruction. However, quite often these forums are not operated in a manner that promotes the spiritual development of its participants. These forums are run traditionally with a banking system methodology that disseminates information, but does not promote critical thinking or self-evaluation. As a result, these forums are unsuccessful at assisting in the transformation of the believer.

Prevalent is the lack of a curriculum that is designed to address both the diversity and the myriad of issues impacting the group participants. The teachers of these groups are usually lay ministers or laypersons that are seeking to gain practical ministerial experience, and are not focused on the spiritual development of those who participate in the group. By default, these individuals are not receiving the necessary theological and practical engagement necessary for their spiritual development.

Regardless of the issues addressed, "mega" churches undoubtedly are here to stay. They are congruent with a world that is fast-paced and highly technological. However, with the emergence of the "mega" church must come a paradigm shift in how the church is operated. The church must maintain its moral responsibility of spiritual maturation of its congregation. If the church fails to uphold its charge, then the church undoubtedly will have oppressed the very ones it once sought to liberate.

To bring closure to this chapter, I ask the reader to feast on these questions: How is it possible to bring the large community of the "mega" church to voice in hopes of achieving self-actualization? How can the educational ministry curriculum be adapted in such a way that promotes diversity as well as address the personal issues of its group participants? Finally, how can the spiritual needs of the congregation be met if the dynamics of the church, as we know it, does not adapt to a highly educated, rational group of individuals that are looking to the church for solutions to their fragmentation? (See Appendix 1 for diagram on learning in community)

On Racism and Human Sexuality

When I was growing up, I don't recall any emphasis being placed on gender outside of the usual language of girl or boy. We all, boys and girls, played together, explored together, and grew together. The one emphasis, however, that was placed on us all was one of black and white. We were taught the way of survival in an all white world (at least the world we knew). We were taught what lines to cross and not to cross. We were taught when to speak and not to speak. We were even taught when to use your "brain" and not to. Racism was real and we were taught early on how to survive it. I must admit that I recall epithets being hurled at others such as "you throw a ball like a girl" or "you walk like a sissy", but I made no serious association with these sayings and gender bias. I never contemplated their effects on others.

It was not until I entered undergraduate school that I was to become aware of individuals that were gay or lesbian and of the purposeful disdain for them. For so long I was in a box, experiencing only white on black oppression, but now I was beginning to look outside the box. I was beginning to realize that oppression had other faces. I observed the disdain, and in some cases hatred, that some had for gays or lesbians, and although I felt inside that they were not like me, I didn't harvest any negative feelings towards anyone of these persuasions. I wondered deep in side how this was possible, a man having intimate affections for a man, or a woman having intimate affections for a woman as one would of an opposite sex. This was a heterosexual society and anything opposed to that was seen as odd. Were these individuals to be seen as odd? Surely, many thought so. I must admit I was numbered amongst them.

Some scholars believe that homosexuality originates from a variety of factors, genetic as well as environmental. (Blumenfeld, pg. 263) There are theological arguments concerning homosexuality as well. We hear biblical arguments which suggest that homosexuality in the bible is not one that is mentioned as a sin, but is one that is only a component of a larger issue of God's disdain for a lack of hospitality. (Deacon, pg. 291) Some defenders of homosexuality in the bible suggest that stories in the bible pertaining to this subject merely reflect the experience of those who wrote it, and are not relevant to modern society. (Gomes, pg. 149) From a secular perspective, we hear arguments such as "ones homosexual or bisexual orientation consequently may be experienced as a source of danger, pain, and punishment rather than intimacy, love, and community" (Herek, pg. 282). We hear also indications that homosexuality is learned, suggested by statements such as "turning bi" (Diehl & Ochs, pg. 279). However, what every argument neglects to emphasize is the humanity of the individuals caught up in this gender war. These are people, nonetheless, with emotions, and feelings the same as heterosexuals. They love, they hate, they hurt, they cry just as any heterosexual. Why must they be condemned to a life of discrimination and oppression?

The answer, unfortunately, lies within a bigger system. The answer is that discrimination and oppression against homosexuals is interconnected with all other forms of oppression and discrimination present in this society (Riley, 473). Therefore, homosexual phobia (homophobia) is a construct, much like race and class constructs. These constructs serve to benefit the status quo, while oppressing and dehumanizing those that are not representative of the accepted norm.

Given the fact that homophobia is a construct much like all of the other constructs in this society, it would seem then that the way to overcome it would be similar to the paths taken by liberationists of both civil and human rights movements. However what is needed first is to examine the nature of homophobia and its impact to society as a whole (bell hooks, pg. 283) If the detriment to society at large is assessed, the hopes of eradicating the oppression are much more likely. But, like all the other liberation movements, this will be a tough but much needed battle, given the history of this and of other nations.

We have all heard of the oppression of the Jews in Nazi Concentration camps during WWII, and the devastation reeked on that society. But a silent story of this travesty is the labeling of gays as degenerate and their being marked for extermination (Plant, pg. 302). Evidently, hatred of anyone unlike the dominant power structure of society poses a threat to those in power. This same spirit of aggression is evident in this society as well. Gays are often targeted for physical aggression, often resulting in death. The penalties assessed to the perpetrators of these violent acts are often receive penalties incongruent with the crime (Minkowitz, pg. 295). In many cases, the prosecutors of these crimes are often surprised if the defendant receives a stiff penalty (one that is more congruent with the act of violence). There is a dualism that exists within this society that is lenient to "gay bashers", while prosecuting to the fullest extent of the law the same crime committed on heterosexual individuals by heterosexual individuals. Something must be done. This world must embrace a legislative posture that protects the rights of human beings as a whole and eliminates inconsistencies in justice. It is not our role to judge individuals based on sexuality or sexual preference. Our role should be to demonstrate love, concern and compassion towards all. We are to show the love of Christ to all and allow the transforming power of the Holy Spirit to minister to those that are contrary to His essence.

There are those that feel that their role in society is to, as the bible states, assume absolute dominion or stewardship over everything on the earth. Whether one sees his/her role in society as one who is to assume dominion over all the earth or to assume stewardship over the earth, there is no doubt that the bible calls humankind into responsibility in regards to the earth. We must be in relationship to the earth. Therefore, every effort must be made to obtain a delicate balance between ecology and humankind. Mutual respect must be shown for nature as well as for every diverse group within society.

It is the norm of this society to heap all the waste of the dominant group upon those that it deems unlike them. It is the practice of corporate America to impose an institutional method of oppression and discrimination on the underclass in general and African Americans in particular. Chemical plants and toxic waste plants are often located in black communities while, the white communities are maintained at the highest level of comfort and safety. What this society has done is to create a class that it intends to step on and hold downtrodden for infinity, in order that their status of security can be maintained. It is a must that all groups regardless of gender, sexual orientation, or class, work diligently to rid this society of the injustices directed toward those not of the dominant group (Lees, pg. 306). Unity as well as cooperation must exist between these groups, and no notion of division must be allowed to occur. It is a must that oppressed groups do not discriminate against and seek to oppress other oppressed groups (Lim Hing, pg. 298). An active unified approach is needed in order to right the wrongs those oppressed are being subjected to.

Self-inflicted wounds: Our attitude towards sexuality and gender identity-based cultures

The Impact of the Extra-Marital Affair and the Down-Low Lifestyle (Non-ID MSM) on the African American family and community

African-Americans, descendants of slaves brought to this continent against their will, are a vast community of individuals whose character, substance, and demeanor has been shaped by adversity. As a result of some 246 years of active, state-sanctioned and government approved slave labor, the position of the African-American within the social economic structure of the American society was seemingly fixed into a minority class, and all but labeled outcasts.

These 246 years of active slave labor were followed by dissension, hate, social and economic oppression, and a milieu of psychological attacks, all perpetrated by those who gained from their status as property. These attacks served to further denigrate a race of people. The attacks have crippled them emotionally and psychologically, so that even if they were able to etch some means of support for their families and communities, the emotional structure of these families and communities would be so devastated. It would truly take a miracle for any member of the group, nevertheless a community of them, to rebound and achieve any status of decent living and to build a family that was emotionally, psychologically, and socially healthy.

Nevertheless, despite the odds, African-Americans continue to make great strides economically, socially, and psychologically. They have managed to raise themselves and their status of living beyond that of slavery, and have become a community that is vital not only to the health of a community, but to the health of an entire nation.

Representing only 12.3 % of the US population (US Census, 2000), the African-American family and African-American community has managed to make great strides when compared to the remainder of the US population. For instance, since 1980 the median family income for African-American families have risen 2.51 times, this is marginally ahead of the median family income growth for all families within the US (demonstrating 2.33 times the 1980 median family income) (US Census, 2000). In addition, the level of education of the African-American has increased 1.96 times its 1980 level for college graduates compared to a 1.57 times increase for the total population (US Census, 2000).

Although these figures demonstrate growth within the African-American community, as well humongous strides made when viewed against the backdrop of slavery and its devastating effects, the African-American community still has many psychological hurdles to leap and many emotional oceans to cross, in order to fully differentiate into a healthy community. The community is still faced with high black on black crime, high unemployment rates, as well as a high single-parent family rate. Nonetheless, it has been the hurdles and obstacles overcome by this racial group throughout the ages that has made it resilient, tough skinned if you will, enabling it to continually make great strides and bounds.

A central strand of this resilient community has been its family structure. Although still faced with many obstacles, it has been the strength and resilience of the African-American family that has continued its survival within the borders of these United States. The African-American family structure, with some 47% of it headed by female single parents is devoid of a biological male father/husband presence. It does not mirror closely the cultural traditional family of the United States with a mother, father (who traditional leads the family), and children who are progeny of the parents. In contrast, the African-American family of the day is one that is substantiated and structured under the traditional African proverb that states, "It takes a village to raise a child".

The African-American family structure has as its strengths "strong kinship bonds, strong work orientation, adaptability of family roles, high achievement orientation, and strong religious orientation" (Nancy Boyd-Franklin, "*Black Families in Therapy*, 1993). This subset of strengths has enabled it to survive. However, to its demise, it is these same strengths that have led to the family falling short emotionally and psychologically, not fully differentiating and as such, glaring symptoms of structural stress (black on black crime, high rate of teenage pregnancies, high incarceration rates, and high HIV infection rates) are beginning to manifest within it. It is the family system that is beginning to show the signs of the many years of adversity, oppression, and discrimination. Unless it is treated effectively, it will suffer a setback much akin to the days of slavery.

I like to take a moment to delve into one of these symptoms of family distress—Non-identifiable, Men Sleeping with Men (Non-ID, MSM), which is most commonly known as Men on the Down Low. In the light of some 48% of the new HIV infection cases diagnosed in heterosexual African-American women, and the fact that the overall HIV infection rate within the United States has decreased tremendously with the onset of new HIV therapies, there is something going on in the African American community that could potentially destroy a generation. Let us address what I view as a potential symptom bearer (something that is an indicator of a larger problem) that has given rise to these frightening statistics. Let us look at the impact of the Down Low lifestyle on the African American male; his family and community.

It is common and understandable that within the African-American community there is an unspoken rule that a boy must display the strength of a man at all times. He must do "manly" things. He mustn't cry, for it is taken as a sign of weakness. He must play with dolls in secret if he is to play with them at all, for it too will be taken as a sign of weakness and will result in him being label "queer" or "gay", both of which are terms within the African-American family that indicates weakness and threatens the survival of the family unit. As a result of this unwritten rule within the African-American family, it is not difficult to understand why secrets, known only to the family, would exist. After all, if the family or any individual within it was deemed as weak, it would bring disgrace to them as well as to the community as a whole. Family secrets, therefore, have become an acceptable norm for African-American families (Nancy Boyd-Franklin, "*Black Families in Therapy*", 1993). They have become acceptable evils, that, although are destructive and dangerous to the individual and family in the long run, must not ever be revealed for risk of judgment.

It is not uncommon for secrets within African-American families to be kept and passed down across generations. "They are often unconscious, obscure, or nebulous" (Nancy Boyd-Franklin, "*Black Families in Therapy*", 1993). They eat away at the very fabric of the African-American family, and unless identified and appropriately treated will ultimately lead to ruin.

For a young boy growing up in an African-American family, pressure is felt for him to be manly, for him to demonstrate the strength of his fathers. For surely, if his father, grandfather, great-grandfather, etc. could undergo the pressures of a discriminative and oppressive society and still raise a family, he cannot be the risk becoming the weak link in the family chain. For a young boy growing up within an African-American family, it is a rite of passage, if you will, for him to reach manhood and to be seen as a strong, stout, responsible, dependable individual who is able to continue the legacy of his fathers, and raise and support a family of his own. It is what is expected, in fact, it is what is demanded of him. He cannot be anything less.

Hetero, Homo, & Bisexuality

Issues of gender and sexuality are most pervasive within American society. In fact, "Gender is so pervasive that in our society we assume it is bred into our genes. Most people find it hard to believe that gender is constantly created and re-created out of human interaction, out of social life, and is the texture and order of that social life. Yet gender, like culture, is a human production that depends on everyone constantly 'doing gender' " (Judith Lorber, "*Readings for Diversity and Social Justice*" 2000). Gender is something that we as a society place upon an individual. It is something that through the pressures of society—the pressure to be like everyone else and not different—forces upon an individual regardless of his/her sexual orientation. After all, boys must act like boys and girls must act like girls. It is the right thing to do, some would say.

"Western society's values legitimate gendering by claiming that it all comes from physiology—female and male procreative differences. But gender and sex are not equivalent, and gender as a social construction does not flow automatically from genitalia and reproductive organs, the main physiological differences of females and males" (Judith Lorber, *Readings for Diversity and Social Justice*" 2000). I must say, this is the viewpoint of the African-American family. If you have a vagina, then you better act like a girl, and if you have a penis, you sure better act like a boy.

Proper gender orientation and heterosexuality is a must among the African-American culture, any deviation from it is largely unacceptable. One must not reveal a sexual orientation that is not heterosexual, lest he/she be flogged a thousand times and marked with a scarlet letter. It is a symbol of disgrace to behave, confess, or profess to not be heterosexual.

But what about the issue of homosexuality, same sex orientation sharing intimacy as though a heterosexual relationship. Is it an abomination within the African-American community? Unfortunately, past behavior towards anyone of this nature indicates that it is. There is a homophobia that exists within the African-American culture. It has been something that has been prevalent as far as the mind can remember. After all, as mentioned earlier, it would be, and is considered a weakness, a threat to the survival of the culture itself, a cultural genocide.

It is this attitude towards homosexuality that serves to cripple the African-American family, preventing it from fully differentiating. Homosexuality within the African American community has been long cloaked in secrecy, and individuals have lived lives of denial for centuries. And those cloaked within its secrecy, have been suffocating throughout time, unable to breath for fear of judgment and excommunication from the very family that is their own.

There is another saying, in fact, a popular song within the African-American culture, the words of which are "I need you, you need me. We're all of God's body. Stand with me, agree with me. We are all apart of God's family" (Hezekiah Walker). Nevertheless, while we sing the lyrics of this song, individuals within our very families are feeling trapped within their own bodies, unable to truly express their identity. And it is not only hurting them, it is hurting those who have labeled them as well.

Consider this: "Homophobia inhibits the ability of heterosexuals to form close, intimate relationships with members of their own sex. Homophobia locks all people into rigid gender-based roles that inhibit creativity and self-expression. Homophobic condition (and indeed all forms of oppression) compromises the integrity of heterosexual people by pressuring them into treating others badly, actions contrary to their basic humanity" (Warren J. Blumenfeld, *Readings for Diversity and Social Justice*, 2000). If one were to accept this point of view, then it can be easily seen how homophobia, a fear of same sex orientation, would cause a self-proclaimed heterosexual individual to not reach full differentiation (Kerr and Bowen, *Family Evaluation*, 1988).

Let's consider further, taking a look at Bisexuality. Historically, individuals have sought to categorize bisexual individuals within the category of homosexuality. However, if one were to place bisexuality into the category of homosexuality, it would be a typology that would lend itself to much difficulty. There is a "heterosexual/homosexual dichotomy" that exists. According to MacDonald (1981), there are three interpretations that reinforce the heterosexual/homosexual dichotomy. "First, bisexuality can be viewed as a transitory phenomenon; the individual eventually comes to re-establish his or her 'true' orientation. In this case, the bisexual phase may be seen as a wish to be 'chic' or 'trendy,' or as an indication of disturbed interpersonal relations. Second, bisexuality can be viewed as a transitional state, with the individual shifting from one sexual pole to the other—this is primarily noted in cases where the shift is from heterosexuality to exclusive homosexuality. In this instance, the person who attempts to maintain any bisexual lifestyle is seen as 'fence-sitting,' avoiding a true commitment to anyone, or as a 'pathetic creature' suffering from arrested development and identity confusion. And third, bisexuality is perceived as a denial of one's fundamental homosexual orientation due to internalized homophobia, or one's fears of being either socially stigmatized or socially isolated"(Paula c. Rodriguez Rust, "*Bisexuality in the United States*", 2000). It would be a grave mistake to label bisexuality as homosexuality.

If one were to analyze all three of the aforementioned interpretations, one can discern or ascertain an underlying psychosis that results in projecting one's interpretations or feelings upon another, and in doing, so the receiving of the projector's feelings experience emotional overload, and at some point in their lifespan will begin to exhibit symptoms of stress. It is at this point that they will be presented as a symptom bearer.

Considering all of the aforementioned information concerning gender and sexual orientation and its viewpoint from an African-American perspective, one would undoubtedly arrive at the conclusion that there is an underlying psychosis that exists within the African-American family system. Unless this underlying psychosis is treated, a symptom bearer phenomenon that not only affects the family, but also begins to spread cross generationally (Kerr and Bowen, "*Family Evaluation*", 1988) to affect others could result.

NON-ID MSM (DL Life Style)

NON-ID MSM, Non-Identifiable Men Sleeping with Men, is a rather new classification of sexual orientation used to describe and categorize a group of individuals, whose sexual behavior has been active but lying relatively unnoticed to the mass population for years. It is a sexual category that has been assigned to heterosexual men who have intimate sexual intercourse with other men. According to Census data, 25% of heterosexual men diagnosed with HIV admit to having sex with men, while still maintaining that they are not homosexual.

Historically, categories of sexual orientation have been resigned to heterosexual, homosexual, and bisexual orientation; however, no thought was given to individuals who move across these sexual orientations. No thought was ever given to the possibility that there were men who would not freely admit that they were anything other than the aforementioned sexual orientations. All, health professionals, experts, and the like, merely accepted the normal classifications of sexual orientation, as it is most difficult to clearly determine sexual orientation. After all, people have difficulty trying to appropriately fit behaviors into proper sexual categories, and it is not so much different with experts. "Most experts in the field are also all over the map when it comes to definitions or understanding of this particular human phenomenon. The fact that there are so many definition points to a confusion of terms" (Janis S. Bohan & Glenda M. Russell, "*Conversations About Psychology and Sexual Orientation*", 1999). It would not be until the rise of HIV infections and the nation's response to it, that this new classification of sexual orientation—Non-ID, MSM—would be developed.

Out of the storm of HIV and STD prevention and awareness campaigns, arose a stream of confusion. It had been long believed that the majority of the cases of HIV infection were from homosexual men and/or IV drug users. The awareness campaigns against such behavior had been massive and the number of new HIV cases for these populations were indeed decreasing, however, there was a new statistic that was glaring—the number of heterosexual cases of HIV were increasing. How could this be? Wasn't HIV infection normally confined to those in the designated populations? How could the number of HIV infections in the heterosexual population be on the rise?

Well, there was a classification of sexual orientation working in secrecy, cloaked by the lies of heterosexual men entangled in triangulated relationships. And these triangles of sexual secrecy would not be revealed if it were not for the boldness of one self-professed heterosexual man, married with a daughter, but engulfed in extra-marital affairs with other men. This man was none other than J.L. King, author of the New York Times Best Seller, "On The Down Low" (J. L. King, "*On the Down Low*", 2004).

Troubled by his life of secrecy and disturbed by the rise of HIV within the African-American community, J.L. King felt the unction to answer what he terms his call—a response to move outside of self and to move into a life that was to liberate others from bondage. J.L. was to become the poster boy for NON-ID, MSM, the "official face" of Down Low men.

True to his African-American heritage, J.L. admits to his fear of going public with his sexual orientation. He feared the ridicule and condemnation that would confront him if he went public with the secret lifestyle that he had now been living for twenty five years. He felt the burden of not only the backlash that he would undoubtedly face, but that of his family as well, not to mention other DL men. For twenty five years he had found safety in lies. He lied to himself, to his wife, to the women engaged in extra-marital affairs with him and to the men who were engaged in extra-marital affairs with him. He had found refuge in secrecy.

However, there began to wrestle within him this voice beckoning him to take the covers off of secrecy. J.L. admits battling with this voice, not only for fear of repercussion, but because he was not ready to give up the lifestyle that he had lived. "When I first started on this journey as an 'official' face of 'Down Low' men, I knew that I was entering into something that would change my life forever. At first, I tried to do this work in denial, seeking to expose the behavior without exposing myself. I remember being interviewed by a report from USA Today and asking him not to use my last name in the story. I used the name 'J. Louis' because I didn't want my identity known. And more importantly, I still wanted to be on the 'DL' " (J. L. King, "*On the Down Low*", 2004). This statement in itself reveals an underlying psychosis that undoubtedly needs treatment, for JL or for those in his emotional family system. For even if he was okay with his sexual orientation, the need to live a double life is indicative of an underlying disorder or source of system stress that must be identified and appropriately cared for.

Throughout the entire book, J.L. provides keys to underlying possibly emotional concerns that must be addressed, if he is to function as a healthy individual within society. J. L. speaks of his "heart being heavily burdened" as well as not having anyone "to talk to about what was going on" in his mind. He speaks of "struggling enormously with the discrepancy between my public and private selves." He speaks of the countless "lies" that he had to tell to maintain his lifestyle. He spoke of not being able to go to his pastor because he "didn't trust him". These are all indicators of underlying emotional stresses, that unless addressed, will result in acting out behavior. "A disturbance in the balance of the emotional system, both within an individual and within his relationship system, can trigger the development of symptoms" (Kerr and Bowen, *Family Evaluation*" 1988).

J.L. provides additional indications as to the extended emotional system of which he is involved: "When I talked to my fellow DL friends about the tremendous pull inside me to come and share this message, they sought to discourage me. I felt that no one understood. There was no one to turn to until I met a strong sister whom I instantly connected with, Juliet Dorris-Williams. She offered an understanding ear as I poured out the inner turmoil I was experiencing. She listened without judgment and encouraged me to follow the directive of my heart." (J. L. King, "*On the Down Low*", 2004)

Additionally, J.L. gives an indication that something went wrong in his immediate family system, further alluding to his behavior as a way of relieving the stress of the emotional system. "In high school, she was more than just my girlfriend. After we married, she was more than a wife. She was my best friend, confidante, and running partner. It's difficult for me to fathom how I lied to her, but I did. I walked in the house, after sexual encounters with men, as if nothing had happened. I didn't think of her life, her feelings, and her future. She suffered greatly when she found out." (J. L. King, "*On the Down Low*", 2004).

One can clearly see the triangles, even interlocking triangles, evident within J.L.'s lifestyle. One can, as well, deduce the level of stress he as well as his emotional system must have been under, based on the number of interlocking triangles present. "One relationship becomes intertwined with others through a process of triangling, so that the relationship process in families and other groups consists of a system of interlocking triangles. The triangle is the basic molecule of an emotional system. It is the smallest stable relationship unit" (Kerr and Bowen, "*Family Evaluation*" 1988). J.L.'s behavior, in my opinion, is linked to a destabilization in his emotional system, and his need to form additional triangles is in response to this destabilization—it is an attempt to stabilize his emotional system.

Therapeutic Strategy

A useful methodology for assessing individual crisis is Bowens Theory of Emotional Systems. The strength of this theory relies on premise that it has the "potential to bridge compartmentalization in biological processes and to provide an explanation for what is observed. The concept's potential for doing this rests in its assumption that all the various physiological systems of an organism are part of a larger system governed by operating principles that regulate the various parts that comprise it" (Kerr and Bowen, "*Family Evaluation*" 1988). In other words, the theory recognizes that individuals much like their biological systems; do not work alone but in concert with each other. Therefore, in all possibility, if one member of a system is dysfunctioning it could very well impact the other members within the system. This theory is the progenitor of a new way of addressing psychological behaviors or disturbances. It no longer looks just at one individual as the sole source or cause of a dysfunction, but it looks at the entire system or family network to which the individual presenting, with a psychological or emotional concern in order to assess what is going on within the entire network. The person who presents with the psychological, emotional concern or anxiety is merely the "symptom bearer" and not the sole source of the disturbance.

Within biological systems, other components can shift in order to compensate for a underfunctioning component. Much like biological systems, families or groups can shift as well when they experience an adsorbent amount of stress. When a family system shifts in order to relieve stress, it is called triangling. Triangles within systems are formed in order to stabilize a unit. This system of triangling can continue in hopes of relieving stress felt throughout the system, forming interlocking triangles until stabilization is reached. (Kerr and Bowen, "*Family Evaluation*" 1988) Unfortunately, within this system, the possibly of poor differentiation has a probability of occurring—an individual may not reach full maturity, and as a result, may have poor self-esteem and therefore present as a symptom bearer.

Another methodology that is useful in assessing emotional health or diagnosing problems or potential problems is the genogram, which "maps out the basic biological and legal structure of the family: who was married to who, the names of their children and so on. Just as important, it can show key facts about individuals and the relationships of family members. The facts symbolized on the genogram offer clues to the family's secrets and mythology since families tend to obscure what's painful or embarrassing in their history" (Monica McGoldrick, "*You Can Go Home Again*", 1995).

If one were to utilize these two methodologies in or to develop a therapeutic treatment plan for Non-ID MSM, it would be most beneficial. As mentioned earlier, J.L. indicates within his book several triangles and interlocking triangles. He has triangles formed between himself, his church, and the men he sleeps with. He has triangles formed between his wife, himself, and the men he sleeps with. There are triangles between his daughter, his wife, and himself. There are many interlocking triangles that are at work within his family system.

I am sure as well if one were to interview JL to assess his family structure using a genogram to look back at his family history, it would prove most interesting. I am sure that somewhere in his history, his sexual orientation, or behavior would manifest itself. Perhaps, even one might even find abandonment or abuse within his family history, which perhaps led JL to "act out" his sexual desires aggressively. Experts have shown that individuals who have been sexually abused or neglected seek, to gain control of themselves and there lives by controlling others. Perhaps JL saw his sexual escapades as a means of controlling his life.

Perhaps, even JL's wife was acting as the "overfunctioning" one within their marriage, thereby robbing JL of his identity. And as a way of regaining his identity he began sleeping with men or having extra-marital affairs.

These are all theories as to what the underlying causing of JL's behavior might have been. However, I am certain that if JL and his family were to submit to expert assessment and a developed treatment plan utilizing the tools previously mentioned as well others, one would find that many of the presuppositions asserted would hold true.

The Churches Role

A possible and plausible opportunity for further assisting the African- American NON-ID, MSM is the church. Central to the African-American community is the church. The church itself is representative of the extended family within the African-American culture. It has served as a nurturer, provider, father, spouse, as well as counselor to its members. It is therefore critical that the church is equipped to assist individuals who are experiencing negativity brought upon them by the socially constructive attitudes concerning alternate or alternative sexual orientation.

In his book, J.L. King speaks of his inability to talk to his pastor for a lack of trust. He mentions as well, the spirit of condemnation he would experience from the church. In addition, JL spoke of the judgmental spirit that would be felt if individuals new of his sexual orientation, a sexual orientation that was highly looked down upon within the African-American community and the African-American family in particular.

JL speaks as well about not having "no one to talk to" (J.L. King, "*On the Down Low*", 2004). He speaks about the need for openness, honesty, and trust, all of which led him to feel that he had to live a life of secrecy. JL, by his own admission, was confused. He didn't know where to turn, fearing excommunication not only from his family but from his community and church.

I believe that the church's opportunity to assist in the healing of the African-American community and the African-American family is to begin by addressing the concerns articulated by JL King. The church develops programs to address the concerns of having no where to go, a lack of trust within the church, the spirits of condemnation and judgment. All of these areas represent opportunities for the church.

The church is to be a safe harbor for those feeling that they are lost at sea. The church is to having open non-judgmental arms to all of God's creation irrespective of race, creed, or sexual orientation. The church is to show the love of Christ to all unconditionally.

Larry McCullum

In addition, the church could initiate family counseling in conjunction with state agencies, in order to minister to individuals experiencing emotional and psychological stresses. It could develop wellness programs for the family in order to reduce tensions. The church as well could effectively minister to its congregation through the development of practical living classes, focused on deconstructing the myths surrounding sexuality with society. Sexual orientation classes could be developed that deconstructs and reconstructs the mentality that bisexuality, homosexuality, or transgenderism is a sickness.

All of these ideas could be implanted in the church, and as a result, individuals feeling that they have nowhere to turn can feel that they have the church. They can feel that they are somebody, and that their differences are celebrated rather than looked down upon by those that were giving influence with them spiritually.

In conclusion, the African-American community at large and the African-American family in particular has constructed strong ideals of what it means to be a man. It has well developed notions that a man is to be strong, tough, and the backbone of the family and community. The African-American family has survived a treacherous trans-Atlantic voyage, slavery, Jim Crow laws, segregation, and so much more. It is widely believed that the strength that allowed its survival is the church and the strong backbone of the family, therefore, perceived weakness is not acceptable.

Sadly, all of this has possibly indirectly led to the spreading of a devastating disease that is attacking disproportionately the African-American population—HIV. African-American men with alternative sexualities have thought it necessary to remain secret about their sexual orientation for fear of being judged, condemned, and excommunicated from their very own families, communities, as well as the church. Rather than risk the dreadful possibilities, they decided to remain anonymous and carry out their sexual desires within the confines of a heterosexual marriage, placing themselves and their families at risk.

Nevertheless, despite the obstacles, and the many lives that were ruined, the alternative lifestyle of Non-ID MSM was exposed by one willing participant, JL King. It is from his personal testimony that this sexual category was identified, and health safeguards and alerts put in place in order to prevent the further spread of HIV within the heterosexual population. However, what remains is appropriate educational measures to be put in place to deconstruct the negative social constructs concerning sexual orientation that exists within American culture, and the African-American culture in particular. Therapeutic tools have been developed to assist in developing treatment plans for those desiring emotional assistance. But as a culture we must be deliberate; we must be intent on demonstrating the love of Christ to all of humankind, so that those whose lives are like ships lost at sea can find a safe harbor within their communities again.

It is not our job to fix; it's our job to understand. It is not our job to agree; it's our job to love and receive.

Epilogue

A broader understanding of the cultural and racial context of African American men and their behaviors is needed, if we are to offer healing to that part of our community that is crying out for help. The statistics that we read about, hear about and see endlessly in the media, paints a dismal picture of the minorities as a whole and African American males in particular. They, in a way, desensitize humanity to the travesty that has occurred in the lives of African American men, the African American communities and the nation at-large. If we are to fulfill the mandate of Jesus Christ, the mandate of love for all humankind, then we as a people; we as a church; and we as a nation must confront the realities facing us! We cannot sit back and allow an entire segment of our population to be dehumanized, disavowed, and disenfranchised. We must come together as a family, a nation and as God's people and offer healing to the wounded, just as Jesus Christ would do if he were here in the flesh.

Unfortunately, slavery has had multigenerational consequences and the impact was mental, emotional, cultural and physical, I'm convinced that the blood of Jesus Christ shed on Calvary can break every generational curse and restore the broken and bruised back to their rightful place in community. We must adopt, implement and continue carry out a societal model that integrates the African American male, and all minorities, back into his/their historical belief system! For it is his family and community that affords him the opportunity to contribute positively. The family and his community is the place of his solace, security and sanctity! Moreover, once this takes place, we as a nation will be free to move on towards really being the "land of the free", "the home of the brave" and "the land of opportunity" for all!

Appendix 1

A Model for Teaching & Learning in Community

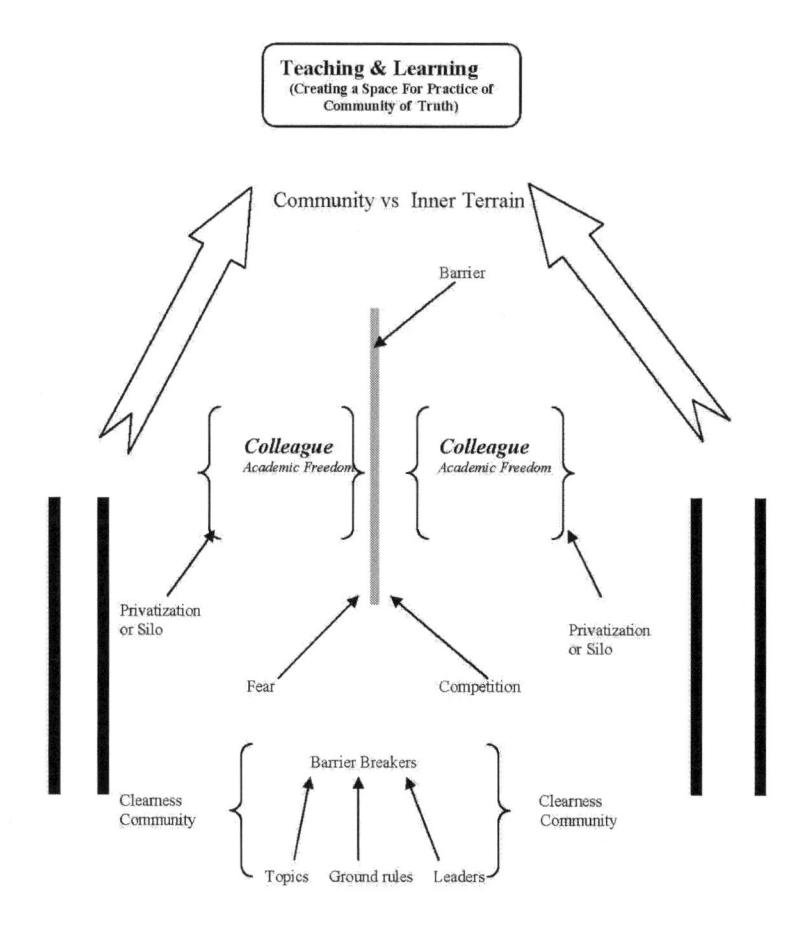

Teaching & Learning
(Creating a Space For Practice of Community of Truth)

Community vs Inner Terrain

Barrier

Colleague
Academic Freedom

Colleague
Academic Freedom

Privatization or Silo

Privatization or Silo

Fear

Competition

Barrier Breakers

Clearness Community

Clearness Community

Topics   Ground rules   Leaders

Appendix 2

A Model for Empowering African-American Men

I. **Attract attention**
   a. Go out of your way! Do something seemingly ridiculous but holy   Authentic display of concern, care and knowledge of what they are experiencing
   b. Speak to the devastation experienced and the internal silent pain
   c. Assure them that there is an alternative—a safe place within a family
   d. Remind that an involved, caring and responsible father can promote healing

II. **Address the absenteeism**
   a. Empower him with the knowledge of his central role in the family, community and socieity
   b. Perhaps your father wasn't there or was there in body only
   c. Teach them that the blood of Jesus breaks the generational curses that have come down their family lines (from their grandfathers and fathers)

The Plight of the African-American Male

    d. Teach them about spiritual warfare and how the enemy seeks to take them out just as Herod tried to take out Jesus at a young age

III. Affirm their value
    a. Provide for the men what they may have missed from their fathers. Tie tying ceremonies are good. Shoe shining sessions done for and with the knowledge of the pastor/mentor are productive. Affirm them speaking biblical stories regarding the power of a servant's heart.

    b. Adam where are you? Insist and prophetic declare that God has need of them in the kingdom, either from the pulpit and/or across the airways.

    c. Encourage them to dream again and recapture the dreams of their youth.

    d. Make prophetic declarations over them for God watches over His word to perform it.

    e. Remind them that God has placed them in a position of responsibility and accountability and that they must pursue and fulfill God's plan for their lives.

    f. Celebrate them (Parade through the church on 4th Sundays or create special celebration days for them)

    g. Give them to make a public confession of their commitment to family, community and socieity

IV. Adopt as Spiritual Sons
    a. Develop a service ministry where men of ministerial promise might work up close to and glean from their pastor/mentor

    b. Develop a program where men have breakfast or an evening meal with the pastor/mentor that they might gather up the pearls of wisdom.

V. **Afford them the opportunity**
   a. We have all missed up at some point in our lives but God is a God of second chances else we would not be saved today. Give men the opportunity to speak in the church and to take part in the church service so that they might utilize their gifts.
   b. Re-enforce to the men that God has given them gifts and talents to be used for the building of the Kingdom! Encourage them to start a business inside and outside of the church so that their entrepreneurial gifts and talents might be showcased.

VI. **Activate their gifts**
Identify and appoint to ministries/groups where their gifts can be utilized.
   a. Develop groups where men can take on active leadership roles.
   b. Develop mentoring programs for the youth, where men who are successful are giving time, talent, and treasures back to the community
   c. Develop men bible study groups so that men might share their experiences with one another and learn biblical principles that they might apply to their lives.
   d. Men are by nature providers and protectors therefore a security ministry should be developed that encompasses all of the bells and whistles of officially trained security that the men might exercise their gifts.
   e. Get them involved in community service.
   f. Insist on them taking a educational course once yearly.
   g. Develop sports activities to integrate balance into the lives of men, i.e. basketball leagues, football leagues, etc.

h. Hold an annual Men's Conferences that is statewide or nationwide so that all men may come and glean from each other, for iron sharpens iron.

VII. Accountability

a. Develop weekly prayer conference calls within the church so that the men might be accountable to one another. Follow-up on brothers who do not call in is essential.
b. Develop a weekly fast day for all men in order to promote unity and accountability to the group
c. Follow-up calls to brothers to remind them of events that are relevant to men are essential so that they might feel and remain connected to the vine.

References Cited

1. Kerr, ME, Bowen, M. Family Evaluation, An Approach Based On Bowen Theory; 1988 W. W. Norton & Company, Inc. New York, NY

2. Kunjufu, J. Black Economics, Solutions for Economic and Community Empowerment, 2nd edition, 1991 African American Images, Chicago, IL.

3. Cole, EL, Maximized Manhood, A Guide To Family Survival, 2001 Whitaker House, New Kensington, PA

4. Friedman, EH. Generation To Generation, Family Process In Church and Synagogue, 1985 The Guilford Press, New York, New York

5. Boyd-Franklin, N. Black Families in Therapy, Understanding The African American Experience, 2nd edition, 2003 The Guilford Press, New York, NY

6. Kornfeld, M. Cultivating Wholeness, A Guide to Care and Counseling in Faith Communities, 2005 The Continuum International Publishing Group, Inc, New York, NY

7. Wogaman, JP Christian Ethics, A Historical Introduction Westminster John Knox press, 1993 Louisville, Kentucky

8. McGoldrick, M You Can Go Home Again, Reconnecting with Your Family, 1995 W. W. Norton & Company, Inc. New York, NY

9. Bowlby 1958

10. National Center for Children in Poverty

11. U.S. Census Bureau, National Center for Health Statistics, Americans for Divorce Reform (www.divorcemag.com/statistics/statsUS.html)

12. Judith Lorber, "*Readings for Diversity and Social Justice*," Routledge, 2000, pg. 205

13. Warren J. Blumenfeld, "*Readings for Diversity and Social Justice*," Routledge, 2000, pg. 271

14. Paula c. Rodriguez Rust, "*Bisexuality in the United States*" Columbia University Press, 2000, pp 11-12

15. Janis S. Bohan & Glenda M. Russell, "Conversations About Psychology and Sexual Orientation", NYU Press, 1999, pg. 131

16. J.L. King, "*On the Down Low*" Harlem Moon, 2004

17. Monica McGoldrick, "*You Can Go Home Again*" W.W. Norton & Co., 1995, pg. 36

18. U.S. Department of Justice

19. The Bible (King James Version)

20. Bishop Donald Hilliard, Jr, Somebody Say Yes
21. Martin Luther Kings Letter from the Birmingham Jail

Additional Works Conferred

Edwin H. Friedman, "Generation to Generation", The Guilford Press, 1985

Margaret Kornfield, "Cultivating Wholeness", The Continuum International Publishing Group, Inc., 2005

Ronald W. Richardson, "Creating a Healthier Church"

US Census 2000

Man Keung Ho, "Family therapy with Ethnic Minorities" Sage Publications, 1987

L. William Countryman, "Dirt, Gree, & Sex" Fortress Press, 1988

Elmer P. Martin and Joanne Mitchell Martin, "The Black Extended Family" University of Chicago Press, 1978

Marcus J. Borg, "Meeting Jesus Again for the First Time", HarperSanFrancisco, 1995

Laura Benkov, "Reinventing the Family" Crown Publishing, Inc., 1994

Larry McCullum

Gary David Comstock, "Unrepentant, Self-Affirming, Practicing", Continuum, 1996

Saba, Karrer, Hardy, "Minorities and Family Therapy" The Haworth Press, 1990

Mark JK Williams, "Sexual Pathways", Praeger Publishers, 1999

Made in the USA
Columbia, SC
21 May 2025